ROUTLEDGE LIBRARY EDITIONS: LIBRARY AND INFORMATION SCIENCE

Volume 14

CATALYSTS FOR CHANGE

CATALYSTS FOR CHANGE
Managing Libraries in the 1990s

Edited by
GISELA M. VON DRAN AND
JENNIFER CARGILL

Routledge
Taylor & Francis Group

LONDON AND NEW YORK

First published in 1993 by The Haworth Press, Inc.

This edition first published in 2020
by Routledge
2 Park Square, Milton Park, Abingdon, Oxon OX14 4RN

and by Routledge
52 Vanderbilt Avenue, New York, NY 10017

Routledge is an imprint of the Taylor & Francis Group, an informa business

© 1993 The Haworth Press, Inc.

All rights reserved. No part of this book may be reprinted or reproduced or utilised in any form or by any electronic, mechanical, or other means, now known or hereafter invented, including photocopying and recording, or in any information storage or retrieval system, without permission in writing from the publishers.

Trademark notice: Product or corporate names may be trademarks or registered trademarks, and are used only for identification and explanation without intent to infringe.

British Library Cataloguing in Publication Data
A catalogue record for this book is available from the British Library

ISBN: 978-0-367-34616-4 (Set)
ISBN: 978-0-429-34352-0 (Set) (ebk)
ISBN: 978-0-367-37635-2 (Volume 14) (hbk)
ISBN: 978-0-367-37640-6 (Volume 14) (pbk)
ISBN: 978-0-429-35537-0 (Volume 14) (ebk)

Publisher's Note
The publisher has gone to great lengths to ensure the quality of this reprint but points out that some imperfections in the original copies may be apparent.

Disclaimer
The publisher has made every effort to trace copyright holders and would welcome correspondence from those they have been unable to trace.

Catalysts for Change: Managing Libraries in the 1990s

Gisela M. von Dran
Jennifer Cargill
Editors

The Haworth Press, Inc.
New York · London · Norwood (Australia)

Catalysts for Change: Managing Libraries in the 1990s has also been published as *Journal of Library Administration,* Volume 18, Numbers 3/4 1993.

© 1993 by The Haworth Press, Inc. All rights reserved. No part of this work may be reproduced or utilized in any form or by any means, electronic or mechanical, including photocopying, microfilm and recording, or by any information storage and retrieval system, without permission in writing from the publisher. Printed in the United States of America.

The development, preparation, and publication of this work has been undertaken with great care. However, the publisher, employees, editors, and agents of The Haworth Press and all imprints of The Haworth Press, Inc., including The Haworth Medical Press and Pharmaceutical Products Press, are not responsible for any errors contained herein or for consequences that may ensue from use of materials or information contained in this work. Opinions expressed by the author(s) are not necessarily those of The Haworth Press, Inc.

The Haworth Press, Inc., 10 Alice Street, Binghamton, NY 13904-1580 USA

Library of Congress Cataloging-in-Publication Data

Catalysts for change : managing libraries in the 1990s / Gisela M. von Dran, Jennifer Cargill, editors.
    p. cm.
    "Has also been published as Journal of library administration, volume 18, numbers 3/4 1993"-T.p. verso.
    Includes bibliographical references and index.
    ISBN 1-56024-516-6 (acid free paper)
    1. Library administration-United States. I. von Dran, Gisela M. II. Cargill, Jennifer S.
Z678.C36 1993
025.1'0973-dc20   93-37279
                                                                                                                           CIP

Catalysts for Change: Managing Libraries in the 1990s

CONTENTS

Introduction   1
   Gisela M. von Dran
   Jennifer Cargill

Empowerment–A Strategy for Change   3
   Gisela M. von Dran

Transforming Libraries into Learning Organizations–
The Challenge for Leadership   19
   Shelley E. Phipps

Education in Response to Change   39
   June Lester

The Time for Transformational Leadership Is Now!   55
   Donald E. Riggs
   Vivian M. Sykes

Managing the Academic Library Through Teamwork:
A Case Study   69
   Susan P. Besemer
   Sarah B. Dorsey
   Barbara L. Kittle
   Carrie M. Niles

Total Quality Management: A Mindset and Method
to Stimulate Change   91
   Janet A. Mullen

Library Leadership: Does Gender Make a Difference?   109
   Paula T. Kaufman

Organizational Change in Research Libraries   129
    Susan Lee

The Maturing Worker in Technical Services   145
    Kay Flowers

The Role of the Collection Development Librarian
   in the 90s and Beyond   159
    Maria Otero-Boisvert

The Budget as a Planning Tool   171
    William K. Black

Index   189

Introduction

The decade of the 1990s is proving to be a period of major political upheaval, economic reprioritizing, and thorough examination of our organizations and ourselves. While the world of education has often adopted business management approaches in administration of educational organizations, the 1990s will be a decade in which not only these management approaches are used in education but we will see our institutions undergoing major restructuring and ourselves approaching provision of library services in ways that are a result of a "revenue diet," technological advances, and changing personal philosophies of our constituents.

In this volume the contributors touch on the role of empowerment, organizational change, and transformational leadership in the evolution of our institutions. The education needed for the 1990s and beyond is examined while we also consider the issue of the maturing worker in libraries and the impact of gender differences. Total Quality Management and Team Management are reviewed and case studies presented. Financial matters will affect our abilities to lead effective organizations, so how we budget will be critical.

The 1980s were a decade of change; the 1990s may be a decade of education revolution. How we deal with this pending revolution will depend upon how well we prepare ourselves and our organizations. *Catalysts for Change: Managing Libraries in the 1990s* provides guidance for the leaders and library staffs of the decade.

–Gisela M. von Dran
Jennifer Cargill

[Haworth co-indexing entry note]: "Introduction." von Dran, Gisela M. and Jennifer Cargill. Co-published simultaneously in the *Journal of Library Administration* (The Haworth Press, Inc.) Vol. 18, No. 3/4, 1993, p. 1; and: *Catalysts for Change: Managing Libraries in the 1990s* (ed: Gisela M. von Dran and Jennifer Cargill) The Haworth Press, Inc., 1993, p. 1. Multiple copies of this article/chapter may be purchased from The Haworth Document Delivery Center [1-800-3-HAWORTH; 9:00 a.m. - 5:00 p.m. (EST)].

© 1993 by The Haworth Press, Inc. All rights reserved.

Empowerment– A Strategy for Change

Gisela M. von Dran

INTRODUCTION

According to a Chinese proverb, if you want one year of prosperity, grow grain. If you want ten years of prosperity, grow trees. If you want one hundred years of prosperity, grow people. The idea of investing in human resources to ensure the progress and growth of societies, organizations, families, and individuals is not original; rather it expresses our collective common sense which has safeguarded the survival of the species.

To secure their own viability and competitiveness in an increasingly global environment, contemporary organizations in the private and public arena have embraced the above philosophy. They are adopting new attitudes and means to manage human resources in order to cope with unprecedented changes in their respective settings. The idea of empowering people is the latest concept used to describe movements to foster the democratization of the work place and the development of staff. Achieving empowerment, however, is a complex process. It is not a short term fix; rather it requires a long term perspective, persistence, and a strong commitment to individual and organizational development. To assist library

---

Gisela M. von Dran is Assistant Professor for Political Science and Public Affairs, University of Alabama, Birmingham, AL.

[Haworth co-indexing entry note]: "Empowerment–A Strategy for Change." von Dran, Gisela M. Co-published simultaneously in the *Journal of Library Administration* (The Haworth Press, Inc.) Vol. 18, No. 3/4, 1993, pp. 3-18; and: *Catalysts for Change: Managing Libraries in the 1990s* (ed: Gisela M. von Dran and Jennifer Cargill) The Haworth Press, Inc., 1993, pp. 3-18. Multiple copies of this article/chapter may be purchased from The Haworth Document Delivery Center [1-800-3-HAWORTH; 9:00 a.m. - 5:00 p.m. (EST)].

© 1993 by The Haworth Press, Inc. All rights reserved.

administrators and employees in their understanding of the complexity of this endeavor, this paper will try to explain the underlying factors for some of the anticipated and unanticipated consequences of empowerment strategies which often puzzle and surprise managers and employees alike.

EMPOWERMENT VERSUS PARTICIPATIVE MANAGEMENT

Empowerment is commonly understood as the process of delegating power in organizations to lower level employees or as individuals' ever increasing ability to use power in order to control or influence their environment and life. The difference, according to Conger and Kanungo (1988), depends on whether the term is used in the management or psychological literature. The first views empowerment primarily in relational terms while the latter sees it as a motivational construct.

A review of the recent popular management literature reveals that the equation of empowerment with participative management persists (Bell, 1988; Macher, 1988; Gandz, 1990; Myers, 1990). It is the new management "buzz word" of the 1990s, hailed as the solution to organizations' productivity problems. This literature lists the usual needs for participatory managerial skills and strategies in the areas of communication, delegation, decision making, problem solving, and resource sharing, among others, as the road to empowering employees. While improvement in these areas will undoubtedly have positive effects on managers, employees, and the organizational climate, empowerment entails more. Those who understand the transformational character of the concept, acknowledge and communicate: a need for fundamental personal development and growth; acquisition of new attitudes and values; increased risk taking; and a long term commitment to redesign the organizational culture to support these attitudes and values. Their arguments for empowerment are linked to employees' expectations that the democratic values we profess will be incorporated in their work environments and that more than productivity is at stake (Bennis and Nanus, 1985; Block, 1987 and 1991; Peters, 1987; Byham, 1989; Kizilos, 1990).

The psychological literature looks at empowerment in terms of self-efficacy, a concept defined and researched by Albert Bandura (1982). His social learning theory proposes four main strategies through which people become self-efficacious:

1. performance attainments;
2. vicarious experiences of observing the performances of others;
3. verbal persuasion and allied types of social influences that one possesses certain capabilities; and
4. physiological states from which people partly judge their capability, strength, and vulnerability.

As one would expect, performance attainment has the most powerful influence because it provides feedback after actual mastery of experiences. Success breeds success. Observing similar others perform successfully is almost equally as effective in learning new skills or behaviors. Verbal persuasion appears most successful if people have already a perception that they are capable of performing the required tasks, the expectations are realistic, and they trust the people who try to persuade them to stretch. Lastly, people will overcome anxiety and fear of failure by learning to acknowledge these fears yet persisting in trying out new behaviors because they rationally know that the chance of success is a real possibility.

Successful case studies of empowerment in organizations confirm that leaders basically used self-efficacy strategies with employees. They instilled a "can do" attitude in their employees, provided opportunities to acquire new skills in a low risk environment, gave positive feedback and acknowledgement for successful performance and acted as role models for desired behaviors (Kanter, 1983; Bennis and Nanus, 1985; Tichy and Devanna, 1986; Block, 1987; Conger, 1989).

Developing self-efficacy in employees, however, is not enough to empower people in organizations just as participative managerial strategies do not suffice. Bandura (1986) found that people who believe in their self-efficacy can still refrain from acting in certain situations because they have observed negative or unresponsive reactions to their own or others' behavior. The implications for organizations are obvious. To effect true empowerment, the management and psychological construct need to be integrated since only employees can transform their consciousness, beliefs, and attitudes, thereby increasing their sense of self-efficacy while only management can start the process of sharing information, material resources and power which will create genuine opportunities for employees to practice new skills and competencies. As tangible results are achieved, rewards must follow. Organizations have to design environments which reinforce the new behaviors of employees, provide competent role models, and help people to remember their self-efficacious behavior, while acknowledging their fears of failure or success.

RELATIONSHIP OF EMPOWERMENT TO ORGANIZATION THEORY

Our understanding of organizational behavior has evolved from viewing people as instruments/objects to be used for the achievement of organizational goals to understanding them as active, complex, empowered participants who constitute the essence of organizations and who create their own social reality. Research on organizational behavior has confirmed that human beings come together in organizations for far greater and more numerous purposes than those articulated in goal and mission statements. Because of the disintegration of the "old world order" of the industrial age, organizations today have become a primary place in society where adults are experiencing major life challenges, and where they come together to acquire and practice the skills needed to master themselves and their environments. Rather than experiencing these processes in reaction to organizational realities, the latest theories propose that we use organizations to facilitate and foster these developments. Healthy human beings develop from passivity and dependence towards activity and independence, culminating in voluntary interdependence to achieve common goals. Organization theories, developed to help us understand and manage the behaviors of people, chronicle an increasing movement towards the empowerment of individuals by placing the locus of control inside rather than outside the employee. They tell us that most employees are naturally self-motivated and do not need constant probing and close supervision.

Expanding our thinking beyond traditional concepts of organization theory, the interpretive and critical organization theories examine larger existential and moral issues. Organizations are primarily viewed as social constructs which need to be changed or transcended to improve the human condition. Proponents of these theories like Gibson Winter, Michael Harmon, Jurgen Habermas, and Ralph Hummel believe that individual and organizational interests exist in fundamental tension with each other and that hierarchical structures and bureaucracies are inimical to human existence. Their theories are developed to help us see organizations as a means to increase human self-understanding and responsible autonomous action. Interpretive and critical theorists differ from main stream organization theorists because their major goal is to assist individuals in their struggle for freedom and meaning rather than in primarily achieving organizational goals. They admonish us to expand our view of employees to include a moral perspective, because human struggle towards freedom is only partially conscious and current bureaucratic organizations defend themselves against any expansion of consciousness (Harmon and Meyer, pp. 299-322).

Since the beginning of this century organization theorists have been at the forefront of challenging our views on the human condition and reality at work. Actual managerial practices have not kept pace and as a result we see much frustration, conflict, and disengagement from work. Now we find that business as usual can no longer sustain us. We appear to be backed against a wall and there seems no way out, except to truly start acting on our belief that human beings are the most valuable resource in organizations. Empowerment may just be the managerial strategy which will yield results.

In an increasingly changing, interdependent, and complex world, it appears inevitable that human beings will need to become creative participants in their own lives and define their own roles in organizations. As democratic ideals assert themselves and flourish world wide, people everywhere will expect that the same democratic principles will be incorporated and practiced in their work lives. Most individuals spend the majority of their waking hours at work and it is there that they are forced to encounter themselves in relationships with others. Facilitating these encounters so that interactions become constructive and assist each individual in gaining self-knowledge and increasing self-efficacy is a challenge. As our understanding of human beings is constantly increasing in sophistication, so must our understanding of organizations. The need for international competitiveness in the private sector and responsiveness and accountability in the public sector is forcing us to redefine organizational reality as the combined processes of individual lives. The movement towards empowerment is a desirable outgrowth of this redefinition, even if it is still largely motivated by a profit or bottom line mentality. We are truly engaged in a paradigm shift with all of its associated conflicts, dramas, struggles, and tensions. To assist us in this transition, we need the contributions, viewpoints, experiences and talents of as many individuals as possible. Only people who believe that their experiences are valuable and respected will be motivated to contribute and those beliefs can be realized through empowerment.

FACTORS INFLUENCING EMPOWERMENT IN ORGANIZATIONS

Power—which derives from the Latin word *potere* "to be able"—has been of interest to philosophers and thinkers throughout history. Many perceived the need for power as an innate drive beyond explanation. Psychologists propose that the need for power can be explained by theories based on compensatory motives or by theories which perceive power to be an important outcome of developmental processes. Alfred Adler was the first to view the striving for power as a compensation for organic or other imagined defects. To overcome this 'inferiority complex,' the mentally healthy person will try to master these feelings through accomplishments (Adler, 1929). Karen Horney argues similarly, except she distinguished between normal and neurotic striving. Normal striving for power is based on a person's realization of his/her superior strength, be it physical strength or ability, mental capacities, maturity or wisdom. Neurotic striving for power serves as a protection against anxiety, helplessness, and the danger of feeling or being regarded as insignificant (Horney, 1964).

While the compensatory theories provide important insights, the developmental theories of intra-personal power appear more appropriate for the understanding of the empowerment process. Sigmund

Freud, and later Erik Erikson, David McClelland and others, described human beings as passing through a number of ego developmental stages. They viewed human beings' orientation to power and the intensity of this need as the outcome of a gradual developmental process during which they learn how to cope with their sexual and aggressive drives and empower themselves to master their environment (Freud, 1926; Erikson, 1963; McClelland, 1975).

McClelland (1975) developed a four stage classification system, to explain which human developmental stages correspond to experiences and expressions of the power motive. It describes the process of increasing empowerment in human beings from dependency on others to voluntarily giving up one's ego in service to a higher ideal. During the first stage human beings typically perceive themselves as strong because of the support they receive from a powerful 'other' like the mother or another caretaker. People who fail to develop significantly past this stage often are perceived as passive and dependent. They align themselves with important others in organizations on whose strength they draw. If other people cannot or will not provide these strengths, they may become dependent on drugs or religion in order to achieve their goal of feeling powerful or special. In organizational terms, such people will do best where they can serve powerful others.

As people mature into the second stage of development, they learn to assert their own will primarily by learning to control their body functions. They experience themselves as a source of strength independent of other people. Employees with a stage two power orientation try to find sources of strength in themselves by controlling and developing themselves and by amassing status symbols. They accrue potential power which they can later use to influence others. They exhibit both aggressive and submissive behaviors depending on whether they deal with subordinates or superiors. They enjoy creating rules, regulations, and procedures to delineate and circumscribe the limits of authority, especially those of other people. The use of physical resources or position power becomes an important pattern of asserting themselves over others. Their need to control themselves may degenerate into obsessive compulsiveness.

During the third developmental stage identified by McClelland, people's energies become outwardly focussed. They find that they can make things happen in their environment by asserting themselves physically or by using more subtle techniques like persuasion, bargaining, and manipulation. People operating in this mode are competitive and strive to succeed by overpowering others with their expertise, resources, wit, intelligence, and prowess. Success in organizations is highly dependent on the effective use of this power style which has been consistently rewarded in Western societies. McClelland identified, however, another type of behavior which is associated with this stage and is used by people who try to dominate others by helping them. It is a strategy more often used by women with high power needs who nurture others with the aim of controlling them or establishing their own superiority.

Lastly, stage four of his model describes the use of power of people who have achieved a high level of development. They have given up the use of power as a source of ego gratification and start viewing themselves as instruments of a higher moral authority on whose behalf they influence and serve others. Cooperation and mutuality replace individual concerns and personal goals are sublimated for the common good.

McClelland found in his research that gender is a key variable in determining how the power drive is expressed (McClelland, 1975, p. 81). Since librarianship is a women profession this finding is significant if empowerment strategies are to be successful in libraries. It is supported by the increasing research, since the late 1960s, on different aspects of women adult development stages. A basis for much of the research that followed, Carol Gilligan's book *In a Different Voice: Psychological Theory of Women's Development*, analyzes the gender differences in development in terms of moral development, conflicts, and choices. According to Gilligan, for men the developmental tasks of achieving intimacy and generativity are preceded by defining their separate identity, while for women these tasks seem to be fused and intimacy develops simultaneously with identity, since the female comes to know herself through relationships with others. Using Kohlberg's six-stage Scale of Moral Development, Gilligan found that women's moral development appears arrested at the third stage where morality is defined in terms of goodness and helping others (Kohlberg, 1958). Women seem to be only capable of progressing beyond the third stage if they start to pursue traditionally male activities which subordinate relationships to rules and rules to universal principles of justice (Kohlberg, 1969). Although later research confirms Gilligan's findings, the women's rights movement during the last three decades has changed women's perceptions of themselves and challenged traditional expectations of self-sacrifice for the benefit of others. A desire for more independence, a balance between self and others, changing relationships with parents, spouses, and children, and the integration of work in women's life appear to be major themes in women's developmental research (McLean, 1980; Michael, 1981, Krogh, 1985).

McClelland (1975), based on research with children's fairy tales and individuals, identified culture as another variable which influences the way people experience and develop feelings of power and efficacy. The effects of this variable are gaining in significance for managers as the workforce in this country diversifies.

POSSIBLE CONSEQUENCES OF SUCCESSFUL EMPOWERMENT FOR EMPLOYEES AND LIBRARIES

Empowerment as a managerial strategy, it appears from this review of the literature, is a more complex undertaking than simply sharing the power that was previously thought to be concentrated at the top of the organizational pyramid. Potentially it has profound implications for the lives of people one wishes to empower, for administrators, for organizations and for society as a whole.

The management literature generally assumes that empowerment will provide employees with long denied opportunities to apply their energy, knowledge, and expertise to the achievement of organizational goals and to develop their competencies. It is thought to foster the integration of individual and organizational needs, increase productivity, and improve the organizational climate through the democratization of the work place. Organizations, however, are comprised of individuals who find themselves at different stages in their development and who generally have little awareness of these stages. They are often faced with a situation where a positive outcome not only depends on their task-related skills and motivation to succeed, but also on their interpersonal skills, level of maturity, mental and physical health, in other words, the whole person.

Until fairly recently, the work force was primarily comprised of men, who were able, largely through informal means, to educate each other about the values of the organization, its expectations, goals, and ranges of acceptable behavior. Younger employees were empowered through mentoring by others or by adopting role models of their own. These processes were for the most part unconscious and not deliberate. But managerial assumptions about how organizations and individuals work are still largely based on that traditional male experience. The increasing diversity of the workforce, however, challenges those assumptions and empowerment may be very different for each person depending on their perception of self-efficacy, their stage of maturity, their gender, and cultural backgrounds.

Libraries, for example, employ mostly women who may satisfy their need of feeling powerful by associating with powerful others or through self control. They may not be willing or able to make relationship sacrifices to become more competitive or influence others, rather, they may prefer to devote their energies to building personal relationships that will make them feel strong. Administrators have traditionally rewarded the majority of employees for remaining dependent or control oriented. They expected people to sacrifice their self-interest for others and give up their assertiveness for the authority of the system. Changing those expectations will be a difficult and long time endeavor.

Assisting employees to become self-efficacious or empowered is likely to be a long term process. Most psychologists and psychiatrists spend years to help clients to achieve that particular goal. Adults in the work force who have not managed to move to the second developmental stage outlined by McClelland have most likely sought out library cultures and positions where their need for external direction is met. They may develop high anxieties, fear of failure, depressions or other illnesses in order to avoid increased responsibility.

If empowerment strategies are successful, they may start to feel over-confident as they experience their increased self-efficacy wanting more power before they are able to understand and handle the associated responsibilities. They may expend most of their energies developing self-control or they act out their newly acquired assertiveness by challenging authority, by becoming excessively rule oriented or by defining the limits of others' authority.

Since libraries and other organizations have generally rewarded competition through promotions, supervisory positions, salary increases, empowering all employees to act competitively, may lead to disappointments and a drop in motivation if expected rewards are not forthcoming. Also, as employees become more self-efficacious, they are more likely to develop their own expertise as a source of power and their organizational commitment may diminish and be replaced in favor of professional association and developmental activities. They are less likely to stay with any organization over long periods of time, rather they will take their expertise where needed and rewarded. People who can be empowered, will become increasingly self-motivated and as they mature, assume leadership positions.

Human resources are proclaimed to be the most important asset of organizations. Their importance has consistently increased as we are changing from an Industrial to an Information Society which relies on the technical, human relations, and conceptual skills of people rather than on material resources to accomplish organizational goals. Progressive administrators and managers are experimenting with innovative approaches to motivate a more educated, diverse, and demanding workforce. They are starting to pay attention to the material, intellectual, psychological, and spiritual needs of their employees and are trying to create organizations which foster individual development. People as well as organizations are in constant transitions and administrators are always looking for new techniques to help them manage an increasingly complex work force. Most of these techniques have benefits as well as unexpected consequences. They will work with some, but not with others and since they are not universally effective, managers may get frustrated and look for something better. Since most management literature reports mainly the positive effects of empowerment on employees, innovative managers have little help in trying to make sense of the unexpected results. They resort to blaming themselves, the employees, the superiors, or the system rather than viewing increased conflicts and problems as a natural outcome of the new power distribution in their organizations or unit.

Empowerment takes more time and effort on the part of managers. Kanter (1986) points out that most innovative managerial approaches demand more absorption in work. This is not only because organizations impose more responsibilities on people but also because many employees enjoy the challenges of more interesting work and participative problem solving. Management tasks become more difficult and time consuming, because it takes more time to sell ideas than to order implementation.

If empowerment strategies are successful, the initial positive results and feelings created by a shared sense of self-efficacy will probably lead employees to push for more authority and to engage in overt power plays with managers and other competitors. While this is to be expected, administrators often react defensively and see this development as a threat to their own authority. Rather than using such power struggles as opportunities to communicate about the nature of organizational and personal power, its usefulness, its limits, its characteristics, and its associated responsibilities, managers may get angry and resort to more traditional management styles.

Employing empowerment strategies will upset the organizational equilibrium and threaten the comfort zones of those unwilling to change. Old expectations, assumptions, and ways of doing things will be challenged and conflict will increase. Employees who were comfortable with and worked well under traditional expectations may react negatively to the new responsibilities, risks, and time requirements of participation and decision making. The more diverse the work force, the higher the level of conflict which is to be expected.

Absenteeism may rise for those unable to cope with change or increased responsibility. Illness appears to be an acceptable way to disengage from work responsibilities and if most employees are at stages one and two of McClelland's model, the work groups may reinforce this maladjustment by providing sympathy and support, and by blaming the managers for being too demanding. Turnover will likely increase as those employees who cannot be empowered leave the organization. Those who internalize their increasing self-efficacy will start the process of self-empowerment by developing themselves and thereby gaining expert power. The organization may not need their new expertise and employees will find better "fits" between their needs and those of the organization.

As a result of these consequences the hoped for productivity increases or efficiency savings will most likely not materialize for some time. If managers are not prepared for these outcomes and failed to create an awareness of these short time losses in those they are accountable to, pressures to abandon empowerment efforts will probably be mounted. Managers need to be highly committed and imbued with a strong sense of purpose to proceed in light of these obstacles. Building a support group and effective communication with higher ups and peers may sustain the momentum for continuation.

In order to truly empower employees, managers have to have high levels of self-awareness, self-assurance, flexibility and knowledge about their employees. McClelland (1975) suggests that people in order to build better organizations need to have matured through the stages of dependency, have taken control of their lives, developed egoistic assertiveness–and then abandoned it–realizing its ultimate unimportance; in other words, effective managers will have moved through the four stages of power orientation. Since this developmental process appears to be dependent on age, gender and culture, we may assume that women managers and those of diverse cultural backgrounds will approach empowerment differently. The question also arises if those managers whose power orientation is primarily at the stage two or three level, can effectively empower others, since their personal power needs are primarily directed towards control and competition rather than sharing. This is important in light of the fact that modelling the behavior of others is one of the four self-efficacy techniques identified by Bandura. Employees are astute in recognizing when words and deeds do not match and increasing cynicism will not contribute to the development of the trust necessary for people to take the risk of trying out new behaviors, stretching from dependent positions into self-assertiveness, or aligning their personal goals with those of the organization.

Managers basically have the difficult task of deciding who can be empowered and at what time. In light of affirmative action policies, this is a most delicate and far reaching decision, which nevertheless needs to occur because there are people in the work place who are "stuck" developmentally. This may be a temporary condition because their energy is needed for other life processes, or it is because of intellectual limitations, cultural conditioning, or psychological problems. Constant change, conflict, role redefinitions, power plays and so on will increase the stress level of these employees and some may become dysfunctional as a result. Managers will then have the additional burden of helping those people regain their place in the organization, transfer them to less demanding positions, or even dismiss them if they no longer can make any contribution.

Empowerment of employees has consequences for job designs. Rather than dividing jobs into the smallest, discreet components as was appropriate for the industrial age, managers will need to restructure positions to foster initiative, integration, flexibility, and the acquisition and practice of new skills. Every empowered person will become a manager of something or somebody, starting with him or herself. Both employees and managers will need proper training for their expanding job roles and to identify their personal needs in order to create or find the resources to fulfill those needs.

CONCLUSIONS

While we can expect delays, detours, suppression, conflict, stress, and other undesirable and unanticipated consequences, the call for empowerment in organizations is bound to be realized. If we understand the importance and the difficulties of the task, we will be better prepared, more committed, and more successful. As managers start viewing organizations as a means to assist people in their individual developmental challenges, they will be less frustrated if expected productivity improvements are replaced by heightened conflicts, power struggles, and stress. They will remember that all change is destabilizing, but also energizing. The evidence of disagreements, challenges to authority, conflicts are signs of a healthy and alive organizational culture where democratic values and principles are practiced. Such cultures will foster individual growth and development which will ultimately benefit all of us, because people will take charge of their lives and become part of the solution rather than being part of the problem.

BIBLIOGRAPHY

Adler, Alfred. *Practice and Theory of Individual Psychology.* New York: Harcourt, Brace and Company, 1924.

Bandura, Albert. "Self-Efficacy Mechanism in Human Agency." *American Psychologist* (February 1982): 122-147.

Bandura, Albert. *Social Foundations of Thought and Action: A Social Cognitive Theory.* Englewood Cliffs, N.J.: Prentice Hall, 1986.

Bell, Chip R. and Ron Zemke. "Do Service Procedures Tie Employees' Hands?" *Personnel Journal* (September 1988): 77-83.

Bennis, Warren G. and Nanus, Burt. *Leaders: The Strategies for Taking Charge.* New York: Harper and Row, 1985.

Block, Peter. *The Empowered Manager: Positive Political Skills at Work.* San Francisco: Jossey-Bass, 1987.

Block, Peter. "The Next Step for Participation." *Journal of Quality and Participation* (March 1991): 55-7.

Byham, William C. and Jeff Cox. *Zapp! The Human Lightning of Empowerment.* Pittsburgh, PA: Dev. Dimensions International, 1989.

Conger, Jay A. and Rabindra N. Kanungo. "The Empowerment Process: Integrating Theory and Practice." *Academy of Management Review* Vol. 13 (July 1988).

Freud, Sigmund. "Inhibitions, Symptoms and Anxiety." *The Standard Edition of the Complete Psychological Works of Sigmund Freud.* Vol. 20. London: The Hogart Press, 1926.

Erikson, Erik H. *Childhood and Society.* 2d ed. New York: Norton, 1963.

Gandz, Jeffrey. "The Employee Empowerment Era." *Business Quarterly* (Autumn 1990): 75-79.

Gilligan, Carol. *In a Different Voice; Psychological Theory and Women's Development* (Cambridge, MA: Harvard University Press), 1982.

Habermas, Jurgen. *Legitimation Crisis.* Boston: Beacon Press, 1975.

Harmon, Michael M. and Richard T. Mayer. *Organization Theory for Public Administration.* Glenview, IL: Scott, Foresman and Company, 1986.

Horney, Karen. *The Neurotic Personality of our Time.* New York: W.W. Horton, 1964.

Hummel, Ralph P. *The Bureaucratic Experience.* 3rd ed. New York, N.Y.: St. Martin's Press, 1987.

Kanter, Rosabeth Moss. *The Change Masters: Innovation for Productivity in the American Corporation.* New York: Simon and Schuster, 1983.

Kanter, Rosabeth Moss. "The New Workforce Meets the Changing Workplace: Strains, Dilemmas, and Contradictions in Attempts to Implement Participative and Entrepreneurial Management." *Human Resources Management.* Vol. 25. (Winter 1986): 515-537.

Kizilos, Peter. "Crazy about Empowerment." *Training.* (December 1990): 49-55.

Kohlberg, Lawrence. *The Development of Modes of Thinking and Choices in Years 10 to 16.* University of Chicago: PhD Dissertation, 1958.

Krogh, Kathryn M. "Women's Motives to Achieve and to Nurture in Different Life Stages." *Sex Roles*. Vol. 12. (January 1985): 75-90.

Macher, Ken. "Empowerment and the Bureaucracy." *Training and Development Journal*. (September 1988): 41-45.

McClelland, David C. *Power: The Inner Experience*. New York: John Wiley & Sons, 1975.

McLean, Pamela D. *A Psycho-Social Analysis of the Life Patterns of Five Hundred Educated Women*. Fieldings Institute: PhD Dissertation, 1980.

Michael, Christine N. *A Phenomenological Study of Female Adult Development Through Age Thirty-Four*. University of Connecticut: PhD Dissertation, 1981.

Myers, Lucretia F. "How to Get the Job Done." *The Bureaucrat* (Spring 1990): 78-79.

Peters, Tom. *Thriving on Chaos: Handbook for a Management Revolution*. New York: Knopf, 1987.

Tichy, Noel M. and Mary Anne Devanna. "The Transformational Leader." *Training and Development Journal*. (July 1986): 27-32.

Winter, Gibson. *Elements for a Social Ethic: The Role of Social Science in Public Policy*. New York: Ronald Press, 1966.

Transforming Libraries into Learning Organizations– The Challenge for Leadership

Shelley E. Phipps

Academic research libraries are in the critical process of transformation. They are being transformed from collection centered organizations to access organizations; from repositories of the printed format to organizations that are less tied to place, to paper, and to print. They are linking users to information held locally or available remotely, and empowering users to become self-sufficient information finders. Their mission is not changing–they have always sought to connect scholars with needed information; but the means available to increase the success of that mission are changing drastically with the advent of electronic access. As such, the roles played by the library in the scholarly communication process are becoming more proactive, assertive, and collaborative.

An organization in transformation is in the process of becoming and fulfilling its potential; it is changing from what it has been to what it must be, given the forces within and the forces without. As such the organization in transformation must find a way to build in the ability to continually learn, to assess the environment, to absorb relevant changes important to its mission, and to integrate adapting

---

Shelley E. Phipps is Assistant University Librarian, University of Arizona Library, Tucson, AZ.

[Haworth co-indexing entry note]: "Transforming Libraries into Learning Organizations–The Challenge for Leadership." Phipps, Shelley E. Co-published simultaneously in the *Journal of Library Administration* (The Haworth Press, Inc.) Vol. 18, No. 3/4, 1993, pp. 19-37; and: *Catalysts for Change: Managing Libraries in the 1990s* (ed: Gisela M. von Dran and Jennifer Cargill) The Haworth Press, Inc., 1993, pp. 19-37. Multiple copies of this article/chapter may be purchased from The Haworth Document Delivery Center [1-800-3-HAWORTH; 9:00 a.m. - 5:00 p.m. (EST)].

© 1993 by The Haworth Press, Inc. All rights reserved.

strategies if it is to successfully become self-created and different. The transforming organization learns to listen to its people, to honor their self-worth, to support their growth, to follow their expertise, and to nurture their development.

"In a learning organization, leaders are designers, stewards, and teachers. They are responsible for *building organizations* where people continually expand their capabilities to understand complexity, clarify vision, and improve shared mental models–that is, they are responsible for learning" (Senge, p. 340). Transformation in libraries calls for a transformation in leadership. We need leaders who design and build new paradigms, the libraries without walls; leaders who work with their colleagues to learn, to grow and to develop whatever is needed to connect people with information and learning. They will not build libraries, direct people, or seek power. They will create the learning processes. The new leaders will not see themselves as knowing the way and teaching the followers, they will see themselves as learners, joining others in the creation of the organization that will allow them to continually learn, to change the vision, to shape the future.

As academic research libraries enter into transformation, transitional leaders have turned to strategic planning, implementation of newer and newer technology, staff development programming, collaboration with computer professionals and other outside experts, and espousal and presentation of their own personal vision to guide their organizations through the major transitions stages. These approaches have helped us move with the future and give direction to the complex organizations we manage and have brought us to the brink of transformation.

As libraries become firmly involved in transformation, leadership capabilities necessary for success will change. In the transformational process understanding of the process is what is important. Transformation is a fundamental change in structure, character, or condition. We must form new organizations, not just add on to the old, although parts of the old organization will indeed remain as part of the new organization, *if they continue to serve the purpose of transformation*. The transformational process is a learning process, guided by the understanding of the basic purpose of the organization and where it is going. In the transformation process we are truly learning what the new organization will look like, how it will function, what it will do because of what it can do, and the new capabilities available to it. Leaders will establish the shape and goals of that organization, they will shape and support learning processes and allow the goals and the structure to grow from within.

We will fail to transform our libraries into what they have the capabilities of being—empowering institutions, giving people the means to find and use needed information, giving students and faculty the tools to obtain, evaluate, and add to or extend knowledge: if, as leaders, we focus on the events occurring around us and fail to focus on our basic purpose and why we are important; if we fail to create a shared vision for our organizations and support our own and our colleagues' continuous learning; if we fail to design organizational structures that empower our staff to participate fully in the creation of the future. As leaders our role is to assist, facilitate, and to empower.

In his thorough and enlightening book, *The Fifth Discipline; The Art and Practice of the Learning Organization*, Peter Senge asserts that "The organization that will truly excel in the future will be the organizations that discover how to tap people's commitment and capacity to learn at all levels of the organization" (Senge, p. 4). Senge's idea of the learning organization is precisely what is needed in today's transformational academic research library. Learning about and utilizing his five disciplines provide a focus for developing the capabilities of libraries and librarians to develop the library organizations of the future.

It is impossible to briefly summarize his insightful and innovative book on creating learning organizations. However, I am convinced that his definitions of leaders as designers of organizations, as stewards of the vision not possessors of the vision, as teachers committed to creative tension involved in pursuing the vision and incorporating the truth of reality are key to the successful transformation of libraries in their role as transmitters of knowledge from generation to generation.

I will attempt to highlight some of the important strategies he outlines and will try to relate them to leadership needed in libraries today.

Senge identifies the limitations of present organizations as disabilities which need to be overcome by applying the five disciplines: his chief components of the learning environment. A discipline is "a body of theory and technique that must be studied and mastered to be put into practice. A discipline is a developmental path for acquiring certain skills or competencies" (Senge, p. 10). Disciplines are to be practiced, not learned and achieved. As one practices, one learns what one doesn't know; one grows and strives for mastery. And, "It is vital that the five disciplines develop as an ensemble." He sees that "systems thinking" the fifth discipline, is "at the heart of the learning organization ... seeing ourselves as ... connected to the world ... seeing how our own actions create the problems we experience. A learning organization is a place where people are continually discovering how they create their reality. And how they can change it" (Senge, p. 12-13).

What are these five disciplines and how do they relate to organizations in transformation? They are (1) Systems Thinking, (2) Personal Mastery, (3) Mental Models, (4) Building Shared Vision, and (5) Team Learning.

1. *Systems Thinking* is the process of seeing the world anew, viewing the whole not just the present series of events, using intuition as much as logic in solving problems. Through Systems Thinking we see the big picture with the human actor very much a part of that picture. System Thinking focusses on identifying circles of influence, not cause and effect linear progressions. Systems Thinking allows for viewing situations with a new perspective, seeing how decisions affect the environment and create predictable problems. Systems thinking will help libraries break out of the predictable cycle of problems, change structures and change the way we react to problems. (A detailed analysis of how Systems Thinking works is covered later.)

2. *Personal Mastery* is seen as the organization's "essential cornerstone . . . (its) spiritual foundation." It "is the discipline of continually clarifying and deepening our personal vision, of focusing our energies, of developing patience, and of seeing reality objectively" (Senge, p. 7). Personal mastery is the goal of each member of the learning organization. It stresses individual self-fulfillment, commitment to what personally matters, and support for each person's aspirations.

3. *Building Shared Visions* is the discipline, not of expounding leader-defined or leader-imagined futures, but the discipline of "unearthing" the existing shared vision of all those involved in the transformation. Discovering the "'pictures of the future' that foster genuine commitment and enrollment rather than compliance" (Senge, p. 9). Learning this discipline is difficult for those of us who see ourselves as the special seers, the prophets, who can forecast and predict, and who want the others to follow where we know we should go in order to survive. We are unwilling to join the followers and discover the shared vision–the real vision of where we are going, despite the efforts of self-centered leaders.

We must foster our collective ability to learn, reducing our powerlessness, holding a creative and positive tension between our vision and current reality, increasing our powers of intuition, connectedness, and compassion. We need to openly share, not just our opinions, but our feelings, not just where we agree but where we differ, so that we can learn about ourselves, our intuitive knowledge, and the power within us to transform ourselves and in so doing transform our organizations and our purpose.

4. *Mental Models*–"The discipline of working with Mental Models starts with turning the mirror inward; learning to unearth our internal pictures of the world, to bring them to the surface and hold them rigorously to scrutiny." These models are "deeply ingrained assumptions, generalizations, or even pictures or images that influence how we understand the world and how we take action" (Senge, p. 8-9). Mental models shape our language, our beliefs, our ideas of what is appropriate and inappropriate, what is possible and what is impossible. For us to create the new paradigm we must break these models and crack the mirrors we have created for ourselves, the mirrors that reflect for us the limitations we think we are surrounded by. We must change the language we use to describe what we do and create new metaphors that will allow us to see the bigger picture and the new and empowering means available to us.

5. *Team Learning* as a discipline differs from teamwork in that the focus is genuinely on the learning of the team, not on individual contributions; a genuine thinking together, dialoguing, suspending assumptions, discovering insights together. Preconceived ideas are left behind and the dynamic of the team, the shared growth, becomes

the goal. The ultimate goal of dialogue is to gain new meaning not to convince one another of individual meaning. The ultimate goal of Team Learning is to openly share and build the future that no one individual can envision.

In discussing why we need the five disciplines and what we need to learn within those disciplines, Senge identifies the limitations or disabilities of present organizations as linear thinking, controlling leadership, negative mental models, lack of vision, and individual competition and product orientation. They are limitations evident in academic research libraries today:

> *Linear thinking:* Libraries have tended to be reactive to changing environmental conditions, looking for cause/effect relationships to the problems we have. We have seen serial price hikes as an inflationary issue not as a scholarly communication process issue; we have seen computers as tools to adapt to library processes rather than attempting to understand their full capabilities and let them guide us in how we can use them to meet our goals.
>
> *Controlling leadership:* The participative developments of the 70s and 80s have opened up the management process, but hierarchy has continued to reinforce control and direction from the top. We have changed from Theory X to Theory Y but the ultimate goal of leaders has still been to get followers to go where they think they need to go.
>
> *Negative mental models:* Librarians continue to see themselves as subservient to others, secondary players in the educational process, unable to assert their view of the importance of empowering students to connect to sources of knowledge outside the classroom. They do not see themselves as necessary collaborators having something to contribute that they alone can contribute.
>
> *Lack of vision:* Leaders of the past decades were slow to see the possibilities inherent in the new technologies to achieve what is not presently achievable in the way we have organized libraries, unable to break the old structures that we know are

limiting. Use of the Internet, creation of the NREN, were not prevalent, driving visions during the 80s.

Individual competition and product orientation: We have stratified our staff and set them to evaluating each other's accomplishments within the product orientation. We have not valued their contribution to the vision; we have recognized their ability to follow ours. We rewarded them for being better than each other, for producing more and more. We valued workaholics; we lost sight of balance. Building collections became the goal rather than the means of achieving the ultimate goal. We compared statistics and allowed ourselves to be rated by size and by numbers. We have failed to see the goal as learning, our learning, our clients learning.

Can we really say that learning is the goal of library organizations? Yes, if we can trust our own power, our own dedication, our own knowledge. The goal then becomes paying attention to the inner self of each member of an organization, to discover what will emerge, not to formulate it ahead of time, force its logic on the environment, but to continually change, continually emerge, continually learn. We easily accept that our organizations must become dynamic, must continually change and grow, must adapt and be flexible. But we keep trying to define the steps and letting them limit us. Senge calls this controlling destiny rather than envisioning destiny and listening to our inner selves respond to that vision. Our goal is to get the right book to the right person at the right time, Ranganathan said. Our goal is to provide bibliographic and physical access to recorded knowledge, many of our mission statements said. Our goal is to educate students and faculty to effectively find and use knowledge sources and to create access systems that ensure that possibility, we might say in today's access-oriented library. But subtly, and sometimes seemingly contradictorily, our goal really is to learn what it is we *are* to do vis-a-vis the present vision. If we can see the big picture, and see ourselves as specks on the continuum, we can see that our individual organizations will and should change and that the only real reason for focussing our attention on our current problems is to learn and grow. Our goal is to have knowledge, to learn our destiny; at this point in time we can have pieces of it by capturing it, by storing it, by passing it on. But if we can stretch our vision and see the real goal, how much more dynamic and transforming can our organizations be?

Senge's disciplines are paths to be followed, techniques to be mastered. They are methods and processes that can directly apply to developing academic research library organizations that are capable of surviving and serving the future. Let's examine them one by one, remembering that he asserts they must work in concert with each other to truly transform.

Systems Thinking, Senge asserts in THE FIFTH DISCIPLINE, is the key to integrating all the other disciplines, "fusing them into a coherent body of theory and practice. It keeps them from being separate gimmicks or the latest organization change fads." Systems Thinking helps us to see ourselves as part of the big picture, and "how our actions create the problems we experience" (Senge, p. 12-13). Systems Thinking has several laws distilled from many writers in the systems field (Senge, pp. 57-67; also see his footnote, p. 394).

THE LAWS OF THE FIFTH DISCIPLINE: SYSTEMS THINKING

1. *Today's problems come from yesterday's solutions.* During the past decades we focussed on amassing books and serial publications, convincing our administrations to give us more and more money as materials prices escalated and space and building costs grew. Now a new generation of librarians must come up with solutions to the problems created by the past.

2. *The harder you push, the harder the system pushes back.* Compensating feedback processes, or well-intentioned interventions call forth responses from the system that offset the benefits of the intervention. As we sought more money to devote to serials because of their importance to research, we encouraged and supported a publish or perish environment that took no responsibility for a situation that demanded constantly increasing the library's serials budget to buy back what our own institutions were collectively producing.

3. *Behavior grows better before it grows worse.* Short term fixes seemed to make progress. The development of bibliographic

instruction programs addressed our need to help our users understand and make use of the complicated systems we and publishers had created to store and preserve knowledge. Have we lost sight of the true goal–organizing information systems so that they can be directly accessed without our help?

4. *The easy way out usually leads back in.* If we apply familiar solutions to problems, we may feel good about them, we may receive kudos from our peers, but if they don't solve the real and ultimate problems, we find ourselves back where we started from. Manager intervention in a personnel conflict might seem practical and effective if the manager knows all the jargon of how things should work out. Telling others what to do, however, is not effective, and leads back to the conflict appearing under another guise. Telling staff that they must figure out what to do and lending them support for their resolution of the conflict, a much harder way, may really solve the problem.

5. *The cure can be worse than the disease.* Sometimes "the solution is not only ineffective, it can be addictive and dangerous." Short-term improvements that lead to long-term dependencies are not only bad solutions but they can support continued dysfunctional behavior. Systems thinkers call this "Shifting the Burden to the Intervenor." By relying on vendors to design our information systems without our full collaboration we make ourselves dependent on whatever they come up with. We must demand systems that strengthen our ability to do what we need to do–make the user independent in her search for knowledge. We must become partners in the design of systems, learning the best ways to design systems that deliver information in a way that users can know how to retrieve it, how to evaluate it, how to use it.

6. *Faster is slower.* Our complex organizational systems will find their own rate of growth. Driving people to be ever faster in their change processes, to ask them do more and more with less and less by demanding, cheerleading, intervening with recognition or rewards for speed, for being first, for pressing time, will fail to move them any faster than they are capable of moving. Giving them support to follow their own vision, to use their own abilities for systems thinking, to share at their own levels, will allow them to achieve whatever is the maximum rate of change. Moving ahead

two paces by fiat only to have to retrace steps because of lack of commitment may seem fast but ultimately contributes to a real slowness in the change process.

7. *Cause and effect are not closely related in time and space.* Causes "are the interacting of the underlying system that (are) most responsible for generating the symptoms, and which, if recognized, could lead to changes leading to lasting improvements." Effects "are the obvious symptoms that indicate that there are problems. . . ." Most of us assume that these two are related in space and time. We look for the cause of a problem in the area in which it occurs and within a time span associated with when it seemed to occur. And we apply "solutions" that merely change the symptoms. Many of our problems, as Senge points out, relate to ourselves and our own view of our roles, not to the events and interactions that we define as the problems. This is why focussing on our own learning can be the key to solving our problems.

8. *Small changes can produce big results–but the areas of highest leverage are often the least obvious.* Discovering where an action gains the most leverage is not an easy task, precisely because it is usually not obvious. In times of funding shortages, investing in staff learning and training may not be seen as the most obvious way to get more done for less. Limiting opportunities for travel seen by our funders, the taxpayers, as entertainment and perquisites, is not really a savings. Supporting such opportunities for learning, rather inexpensive investments, may have the biggest longterm payoff for helping our libraries to become ultimately successful. Building collaborations with professionals outside libraries and with our faculty are other not so obvious areas where high gains may be had.

9. *You CAN have your cake and eat it too–but not at once.* Seeing the big picture, viewing the entire continuum, can keep us from making choices that result in short term quick fixes. If we truly understand the goal of libraries as full learning organizations we can invest in creating those organizations and discover what empowers them to create learners of others. We will have to work through the steps of achieving that goal and make "either-or" choices as we go, but in the end, if we keep the real goal in mind, those choices can be opportunities for learning, and we can have our cake and eat it too.

10. *Dividing an elephant in half does not produce two small*

elephants. "Living systems have integrity. Their character depends on the whole." Most organizations are structured to keep people from seeing the whole and keeping them from important interactions because of status, because of hierarchy, because of rigid functional divisions. The key principle to avoiding the slaughter of the elephant is applying the "'principle of the system boundary'... that the interactions that must be examined are those most important to the issue at hand, REGARDLESS of parochial organizational boundaries." Pitting the faculty and the library against the administration, or the vendors against the librarians, when examining a funding issue does not solve a problem. An examination of all the factors contributing to the present dilemma, an open dialogue about expected results, an empowering of all parties to contribute to solutions is a better way to achieve the ultimate goal ... of learning.

11. *There is no blame.* Systems thinking helps us to realize that circumstances outside us, international conglomerate publishers, the research orientation of major universities, the tenure system, the computer gurus, are not to blame. "(We) and the cause of our problems are part of a single system." It is by collaborating with our "enemies" and developing relationships with them that we will ultimately find enduring solutions.

In Systems Thinking then, we must see the forest and the trees. We must recognize the patterns that control events and "change the thinking that produced the problem in the first place" (Senge, p. 95). Systems Thinking, combines with the other four disciplines to move the organization to a state of generative learning, ever improving, shaping, and changing the vision, the structure.

Let's examine the other four disciplines.

STRIVING FOR PERSONAL MASTERY: "Organizations learn only through individuals who learn. Individual learning does not guarantee organizational learning. But without it no organizational learning occurs." Organizations will not change if they don't support and encourage change and growth in their professionals and staff. Personal mastery involves "continually clarifying what is important to us" as individuals, and "continually learning how to see current reality more clearly" (Senge, p. 139-141). When an organization commits to personal mastery it does so, not because any one person will gain, not because it is a means to getting something from individuals but because personal mastery is important to individuals. When individuals seek and practice personal mastery there will be organizational gain, but that is not the goal. The mastery itself is the goal. What does it involve? Finding one's own personal vision, one's own inner sense of self. Personal mastery is a discipline because "it is a process of continually focusing on what one truly wants, on one's vision."

Too many of our organizational members are seeking their purpose from the organization of which they are a part. They become dependent on their job, their status, their accomplishments, to define them, rather than the other way around--letting their vision, their knowledge of themselves define the organizations in which they choose to develop. Continually balancing the creative tension between our vision and our current reality is vital to practicing personal mastery. Delineating between our ingrained concepts of reality and our honest and uninhibited observations is also key. Personal mastery involves a commitment to one's own vision and a commitment to the truth. Often the egotism, the insularity, the parochialism of leadership makes this a very difficult dual commitment. It is too easy to latch onto a popular vision, to ignore the realities that don't fit that vision, to use power to get others to buy into that vision, and to shut out the realities that might change that vision. Honesty, openness, questioning, listening, and sharing are important ingredients in practicing personal mastery. We must constantly get honest feedback about mistakes, misperceptions and accomplishments in order to continue to learn. Creating the organizational structure where this is supported, valued, critical, and expected is key to creating the learning organization.

The systems perspective of personal mastery "also illuminates subtler aspects . . .–especially integrating reason and intuition; continually seeing more of our connectedness to the world; compassion; and commitment to the whole" (Senge, p. 167). Integrating reason and intuition are seen as critical to practicing systems thinking, viewing ourselves and our organizations as parts of a greater, meaningful reality. As we begin to see that we have all been part of structures that have trapped us into becoming separate and limited, compassion becomes a binding force that opens us up to greater awareness, empathy, and learning. These then lead to a "broader vision" and a greater "connectedness to the whole" that can only lead to a greater understanding, and a more productive organization.

MANAGING MENTAL MODELS: Our mental models "determine not only how we make sense of the world, but how we take action" (Senge, p. 175). Our mental models may be simple generalizations or complex cultural beliefs or values, but they definitely shape behavior, consciously or unconsciously. Much research is currently being done in the field of negative mental models, the effects of dysfunctional families on adult children's behavior, the effect of abuse on adult living patterns, the reasons behind addictive and codependent behavior. In that research the key to positive change is changing one's own attitude about the event(s) that led to the development of reactive patterns of behavior. Reacting as victim when one really *has* choices and *can* take action is construed as applying one's own negative mental model of powerlessness. Present attitudes toward past events are influencing continued dysfunctional behavior.

Senge suggests addressing the mental models embedded in the tradition of organizations, encourages examining them in light of reality, changing them in order to move into more relatedness with the world. If deeply entrenched mental models can lead to inertia and impede change, then other models can accelerate learning and encourage action. Cannot changed attitudes lead to more positive behaviors? He uses examples such as developing a world-view of business or challenging the values of hierarchy. He gives examples of companies that have developed ways of breaking apart mental models by:

- Recognizing 'leaps of abstraction' (noticing our jumps from observation to generalization)
- Exposing the 'left-hand column' (articulating what we normally do not say)
- Balancing inquiry and advocacy (skills for honest investigation)
- Facing up to distinctions between espoused theories (what we say) and theories-in-use (the implied theory in what we do) (Senge, p. 186, discussing Hanover's skill building based on Argyris, Beckett, and others).

Honesty, inquiry, self-disclosure. These become the mode of the discipline of managing mental models. In shifting the way we view current structures or events, the way we respond to changes in the larger world, the way we view our own power to shape our future, "the learning organizations of the future will make key decisions based on shared understandings of interrelationships and patterns of change" (Senge, p. 204). They will not be inhibited by the development of new, restricting mental models because processes of questioning, clarifying and redefining will be the models themselves.

DEVELOPING SHARED VISION: "A vision is truly shared when you and I have a similar picture and are committed to one another having it, not just to each of us, individually, having it. When people truly share a vision they are connected, bound together by a common aspiration.... Shared visions derive their power from a common caring.... (O)ne of the reasons people seek to build shared vision is their desire to be connected in an important undertaking" (Senge, p. 206).

In the learning organization shared vision provides the "focus and energy for learning." In order to build shared vision, leaders must encourage personal vision and share their own vision in a way that others are encouraged to share theirs and connect one with the other. An organization's vision will be the sum of the whole; the leader cannot move the organization toward a vision that others do not hold. The organization will evolve toward its own contradictory vision if that is the shared vision. The leader's responsibility then becomes connecting and building the vision through sharing, dialogue, listening and helping others to co-create the vision.

"Formal" and "grudging" compliance to "the leader's vision" are seen as contrary to what is really desired: enrollment and commitment. Even "genuine" compliance is viewed as just "being a good soldier" and formal compliance is just being a "pretty good soldier," doing what's expected and no more. Grudging compliance is just following along so as not to lose one's job. Enrollment is understanding the vision and doing whatever can be done "within the spirit of the law." Commitment to a vision, which really is only possible when one considers it her own personal vision, is wanting it to happen, "creat(ing) whatever 'laws' (structures) are needed" (Senge, p. 219). In suggesting guidelines for enrollment and commitment Senge stresses that it comes from one's own genuine enthusiasm, not from coercion, persuasion, or fostering. "Be enrolled yourself. . . . Be on the level. . . . Let the other person choose." "The hardest lesson for many managers to face is that, ultimately, there is nothing you can do to get another person to enroll or commit" (Senge, p. 222-223).

SUPPORTING TEAM LEARNING: For team learning to be successful "there is a need to think insightfully about complex issues," to tap the many minds, to trust intuition and reason. Also, there is the need "for innovative, coordinated action," and consideration of "the role of team members on other teams." Some of our organizations are used to working with teams, but we may not be using them effectively because we are ignoring some of these guidelines. We are not encouraging the tackling of complex issues, providing members of the teams with the skills to disagree, to address feelings, to break large problems into small parts. We may not be encouraging innovation, giving permission for new ideas to come from teams, expecting creativity from groups whom we have charged with problem solving. Too often we ask them to look at the same tired solutions, to pick one and to recommend how to implement it. We don't challenge them to think of the unthinkable, to step out of the problem and apply processes that open up imagination.

Also, we often isolate our different teams; we don't let them work at seeing they have the information we have, we don't encourage them to cross-pollinate, to work on different levels, to seek ideas from non-experts. Collaboration with outsiders and with key players who are from a different field or background can be a powerful way of increasing the range of solutions and creative ideas available to us, as Michael Schrage has pointed out in his book *Shared Minds,* (1990).

In order to support team learning we need to master the practices of dialogue and discussion, to break defensive routines that serve to cover up the real problems. Defensiveness is considered bad in our culture, and as such is not easily admitted. If we make it all right to admit we are defensive in our organizations, to make defensiveness discussable, we can avoid the control that defensiveness breeds. Self-disclosure and looking for the causes of defensiveness are two possible ways that one can apply the systems thinking solution of "weakening the systematic solution and strengthening the fundamental solution" (Senge, p. 255). Admitting the non-productive behavior lessens its strength; questioning why one feels that way opens the way for more productive open behavior.

We must also ask everyone to suspend their individual assumptions that tend to polarize groups; act as colleagues who share the problem and therefore must share the solution development, and maintain an open atmosphere where anything and anyone may be questioned without creating a threatening atmosphere (Senge, p. 260-261).

Senge goes on in his comprehensive analysis of creating the learning environment by addressing questions of how the five disciplines can "resolve the practical problems and issues faced by the prototype learning organizations." These issues include:

- How can the internal politics and game playing that dominate traditional organizations be transcended? (Chapter 13, "Openness")
- How can an organization distribute business responsibility widely and still retain coordination and control? (Chapter 14, "Localness")
- How do managers create the time for learning? (Chapter 15, "A Manager's Time")
- How can personal mastery and learning flourish at both work and home? (Chapter 16, "Ending the War Between Work and Family")
- How can we learn from experience when we cannot experience the consequences of our most important decisions (Chapter 17, "Microworlds") (Senge, p. 272).

These are crucial discussions and present a firm foundation for moving forward in the creation of the learning organization.

Developing the shared vision and giving people the freedom to work toward it, participating in its development is the hallmark of *openness*. People also need to be encouraged to continually reflect on whether they are participating in something that matches their values, to comment and question, and to continue to create the organization that is congruent with their values. To question one's own values, to share that questioning process, is a sign that game playing and internal politics are not the dominant processes.

Achieving control without controlling involves delegating the responsibility and authority to the *local* level. Continuing the shared visioning process allows for everyone to be on the same wavelength. Team learning skills, emphasis on personal mastery and development of everyone's systems thinking skills allows for local decision-making to be effective and productive. Encouraging risk taking and backing it up by "forgiving" is also crucial to the continuous learning of members of an organization. Giving people the tools they need to move the organization forward and keeping the focus on learning will allow for eradication of the negative morale and lack of self-fulfillment associated with hierarchical control.

It goes without saying that much of the manager's *time* in the learning organization must be focussed on learning—on thinking and reflecting. Much more time needs to be spent in our organizations on "why" rather than on "how." We are often too focussed on answers to the obvious questions rather than on ferreting out the not-so-obvious questions. "Incisive action (should) not be confused with incessant activity" (Senge, p. 304).

"The learning organization cannot support personal mastery without supporting personal mastery in all aspects of life. It cannot foster shared vision without calling for the personal visions, and personal visions are always multifaceted—they always include deeply felt desires for our personal, professional, organizational, and family lives. Lastly, the artificial boundary between work and family is anathema to systems thinking. There is a natural connection between a person's work life and all other aspects of life. We live only one life, but for a long time our organizations have operated as if this simple fact could be ignored, as if we had two separate lives" (Senge, p. 307). Amen. I couldn't say it better!

Learning through transitional experiences (such as role modelling and team building) and the use of microworlds are methods that we have used throughout our learning careers. Microworlds are those playing experiences that modelled behavior, relationships, and reality for us without recreating the total complexity of the culture or the situation: playing store, building with blocks, playing Monopoly. Senge supports using microcomputers to continue this microworld approach to learning. Using microcomputers to "allow groups to reflect on, expose, test, and improve the mental models upon which they rely in facing difficult problems," are new tools for experimenting, getting feedback, assessing the impact of choosing one strategy over another. Playing and modelling are ideal uses of the microcomputers that we all increasingly have available to us. Encouraging the development of skills in their use and the time to play, to model, to experiment will enhance the learning capability of the learning organization.

And what of the leader in the learning organization? What is the role of the leader? What are the skills needed? How are the skills developed? The new leader is the designer of the learning organization, the one who sets the tone, who makes learning the key element of the culture, and who designs the processes that support the goal and mastery of learning. The leader as designer is often not the chosen role of today's leadership. Why? "Little credit goes to the designer" of a ship. The captain gets the credit. And too, "Those who aspire to lead out of a desire to control, or gain fame, or simply to be 'at the center of the action' will find little to attract them to the quiet design work of leadership" (Senge, p. 341). Designers of new organizations, focussed on continual learning and commitment to the five disciplines, are what is needed in today's academic research library.

Leaders also have to be the stewards of the vision, the ones who carry the purpose of the organization into the future. In myriad native cultures the leaders are the stewards, the carriers of the story of the people, the purpose of life. So it is in the learning organization, the leader is the teller of the stories, who instills "responsibility without possessiveness," who keeps the focus on purpose and does not control the way, the method, the means, but empowers others to choose as they remember and continually recreate the vision.

" 'The leader as teacher' is not about 'teaching' people how to achieve their vision. It is about fostering learning, for everyone.... Accepting this responsibility is the antidote to one of the most common downfalls of otherwise gifted leaders—losing their commitment to the truth" (Senge, p. 356). If the leader sees her role as fostering learning there will truly be shared vision, shared commitment, shared progress. There will be a lessening of the tensions created by the we/they attitudes that cause resentment, limited productivity, and endless concern over fixing problems when leaders can truly see themselves as fostering learning.

We have an incredible reservoir of creative, energetic talent in our academic research libraries. Let's seek the leaders that will be designers, stewards, and teachers; who will help us create learning libraries where we pursue the five disciplines for the purpose of modelling to the education environment in which we live, their reason for being. Let's give up the goal of getting information to people and let's assume the goal of creating a learning organization for people who care that other people have information they need and want. This leaves great room for new and creative ways of thinking what librarianship is all about and transforming libraries to serve the ultimate cause of learning.

REFERENCES

Senge, Peter M. (1990). *The Fifth Discipline: The Art and Practice of the Learning Organization*. New York: Doubleday Currency.
Schrage, Michael (1990) *Shared Minds: The New Technologies of Collaboration*. New York: Random House.

Education in Response to Change

June Lester

INTRODUCTION

The effective preparation of those individuals who will manage libraries from now into the twenty-first century requires a professional education that is responsive, both to the changes that currently are occurring and to those that are predicted in the near term. In addition, effective education requires the preparation of professionals who can not only anticipate change, but who also act as change agents, directing and bringing about change in their institutions, in response to societal needs and shifts.

Changes in Society

As an instrument of society, the institution of the library has always been influenced by changes in the host environment; today's library is no different. To understand how librarians must be educated for the remainder of the century, it is instructive to look first at what changes are occurring in U.S. society and what is anticipated between now and the year 2000. For the near term, the course of change appears to be fairly clear; and prognosticators tend to agree,

---

June Lester is Associate Dean, School of Library and Information Sciences, University of North Texas, Denton, TX.

[Haworth co-indexing entry note]: "Education in Response to Change." Lester, June. Co-published simultaneously in the *Journal of Library Administration* (The Haworth Press, Inc.) Vol. 18, No. 3/4, 1993, pp. 39-54; and: *Catalysts for Change: Managing Libraries in the 1990s* (ed: Gisela M. von Dran and Jennifer Cargill) The Haworth Press, Inc., 1993, pp. 39-54. Multiple copies of this article/chapter may be purchased from The Haworth Document Delivery Center [1-800-3-HAWORTH; 9:00 a.m. - 5:00 p.m. (EST)].

at least at a macro level, on both direction and degree of a number of shifts that have potential for substantial impact on the library as an institution. A brief listing would include changes in the following areas, along the dimensions indicated.

Cultural Pluralism and Diversity

Current predictions for the demographic composition of U.S. society by the year 2000 are that nearly one-third of the population will be composed of various minorities.[1] For some states, the projected growth in minority populations is even more dramatic; for example, California is expected to have a majority of collective minorities by the year 2003.[2] Within the various populations, the Hispanic population is growing at a rate that is five times greater than the growth rate of the non-Hispanic population.[3] These differential growth rates will dramatically alter the composition of the school-age population. Even within the Hispanic population, there is considerable cultural diversity. Three major groups compose the Hispanic community: Mexican American, Puerto Rican, and Cuban.[4]

An Increasingly Older Population

By the year 2000, over half of the population is predicted to be 35 years of age or older. Between 1990 and 2000, the numbers of those in the 35-44 group will increase 16.4 percent, the 45-54 age bracket will increase 46 percent, and the 75 and over bracket, 26.2 percent. These changes are even more dramatic when compared to the predicted overall population growth of 7.1 percent.[5]

Increased Variety in the Configuration of Households

If past trends hold, by the year 2000 the married couple household will become the pattern for the minority of households in the U.S., although the number of family households will be larger than that of nonfamily households (approximately 36 percent).[6] Households headed by men will grow faster than other types, with single-parent families headed by men growing 42 percent and nonfamily households headed by men, 72 percent.[7] These changes are reflected in the predictions that by the year 2000, 60 percent of the children born in the 1980s will have lived in a one-parent household, 25 percent will have lived with a stepparent by the time they are sixteen, and in one-third of the households, there will be no children; less than 4 percent of "families" will be the stereotyped working father, stay-at-home mother, and two children.[8]

Changes in the Work Force and in the Work Place

In addition to the changes resulting from increasing ethnic and racial diversity and the aging of the population, the numbers of women in the work force will increase faster than the numbers of men, so that by the year 2000, 80 percent of women in the 25-34 category will work outside the home (up from 70 percent). The numbers of temporary workers, independent workers, part-time workers and "contingent workers" (workers paid only for working, without benefits) will grow faster than other employment categories. The proportion of immigrants in the work force, particularly in such areas as science and engineering, will increase. Continued attention will need to be given to increasing work place literacy, and retraining needs will escalate such that 75 percent of workers will need retraining by the year 2000.[9] As a result of the Americans with Disabilities Act, the diversity of the work place will be further expanded through the addition of this previously underemployed sector of the population.

These changes will generate restructuring of the work place and how it is managed, including more flexible work schedules, greater support for the family responsibilities and obligations of workers, and increased acceptability of and adaptability to differing attitudes, values, and lifestyles among the work force.[10] In addition, the increasing use of information processing and information technology as a job component and the ability to distribute work geographically as a result of advances in information technology will continue to influence the reconfiguration of the work place.[11]

Globalization

Much of the globalization trend is played out in the economic sphere, through increasing competition from other nations, from greater foreign presence in the U.S. economy through ownership as well as imports, and by declining U.S. economic power. The geopolitical changes of the immediate past and the present will continue to affect the internationalization of society.

Shifts in Education

The four-year college degree taken by a person who comes straight from the K-12 experience is already an anomaly, even though this ideal in higher education has been slow to change. During the 1990s, the trend toward older students in higher education will continue;[12] and after a decline in the middle of the decade, total enrollment is projected to increase by 5.7 percent by the year 2000, with the greater growth occurring in two-year institutions.[13] Elementary and secondary school enrollments will also increase, by a projected 8.2 percent, between 1990 and 2000, in contrast to the period of decline in the mid-1980s.[14] Minority populations in the schools will increase proportionately, especially the percentage of Hispanics, although it is questioned whether this trend will continue into higher education.[15] Both the expanding diversity of the population and the globalization of business will lead toward increased inclusion of foreign languages in the schools as well as bilingual instruction. Some even predict a foreign language requirement for all college entrants.[16]

Other changes that are current and predicted to continue that will impact libraries include:

- escalating health care costs,
- increasing environmental awareness and concern, and
- growing numbers of homeless.

Perhaps the most immediate societal fluctuation affecting libraries is the nation's continued economic ill health, the impact of which on libraries is reported monthly or more frequently on the pages of *American Libraries* and *Library Journal*. Stories of "drastic cuts," "staff furlough," "libraries cutting hours," "awaiting budget cuts," and "being hurt by state budgets" are all too easy to find.[17]

Changes in Libraries

At the same time that macro level societal shifts are affecting and will affect the library as an institution by changing the nature of clientele served, the operational environment in which libraries exist, and the nature of the socio-economic and political climate, changes are occurring in the microenvironment of the library. Developments in information technology and structure have altered the technological base of the library dramatically. The shifting information infrastructure is affecting both information flow and the access points for information.

As with societal change, it is fairly easy to find predictions of the library of the future, but not all of them tend to agree. One can readily find descriptions of the electronic library in which even what has been called reference service will be delivered to the individual's work station.[18] In his recent review of predicted scenarios of libraries of the future, however, Malinconico challenges one assumption he finds in many of the future scenarios, that is, that the library in its present organizational and institutional structure will continue. He foresees that technological developments and resulting realignments of institutional information systems "will weaken the influence and importance of central information repositories, i.e., traditional libraries. . . ." He goes on to say that "a scenario in which technology accretes to an organization bearing a continuous relation to the traditional library seems increasingly unlikely. On the other hand, consolidated control of information sources, as well as of mechanisms for access to and dissemination of information, does appear to be a likely scenario." In his scenario the roles of libraries and computer centers will converge.[19]

This view and others that abound in describing the academic library of the future contrast sharply with other indications, particularly with some concerned with where public libraries are headed. A recent study of future directions for public library services, as perceived by public library directors, reveals expectations of continuing focus on traditional services of circulation of books, reference service based on print sources, children's programming, and telephone reference.[20] There was no electronic library, no questioning of the library in its present configuration, no envisioning of the types of information delivery to the home that are currently possible and that indeed have been initiated by some public libraries. Even within the academic library environment, the expectations of those served may be at odds with current capabilities and realities, as well as with the vision of the electronic library of the future.[21]

Regardless of the predictions, certain reality is that libraries are being and will continue to be affected by technological change and the resulting reconfiguration of the information infrastructure. Also certain is that libraries have been and will continue to be impacted by the fiscal vicissitudes of the nation's economy.

Changes in Library and Information Science Education

While predictions are readily available for changes in libraries as the twenty-first century approaches, even if there is not unanimity about what the changes are likely to be, scenarios for library and information science education are not so plentiful. That there have been important changes in the educational base over the past decade is indisputable, even if some of those changes are not judged to be positive.

Most striking, and certainly most lamented, has been the closing of schools with ALA-accredited master's programs.[22] Previously believed to be due to financial exigency and related to local circumstances,[23] more recently the closings have been perceived as potentially an escalating trend, especially in research universities. There is fear that the entire educational structure by which the profession renews itself could crumble or be radically altered, either leaving education for the information professions under the aegis of other areas that have not held the values or the user view that has given education in schools of library and information studies its unique character, or forcing libraries to resort to staffing by those without professional education. Major themes that run through the various analyses and commentaries on the closing of schools are the isolation of the school, the perceived lack of relevance to the central mission of the university, and the lack of political acumen on the part of library school faculty and administrators.[24] Although some may project (or hope) this trend will abate, there are prognostications that it will continue and that more closings will occur, primarily in the research university setting.[25]

On a more positive note (at least to some) has been the widening of access to accredited programs through various distance education initiatives. In 1990-1991, thirty-five schools in the U.S. with ALA-accredited programs offered either part or all of the accredited master's program at a site other than the main campus of the host university; sixteen did not.[26] Such activity is likely to expand over the decade of the 1990's, based on the reported projections and plans of the schools as well as new initiatives actually begun in the 1991-1993 time frame, and will involve an increasing variety of delivery modes and expanded use of telecommunications.[27]

Curriculum changes likewise have been plentiful, many occurring in response to technological developments and the need to provide technological literacy at higher levels, such as addition of courses in database management, user interface design, and telecommunications.[28] Other changes reflect the general shift in the curricula of the schools to a focus on information, not on the building or the institution through which the information is delivered, as demonstrated by expansion of offerings to include courses dealing with information policy, economics of information, human information behavior, and information ethics. That curricula activity in schools with accredited programs is extensive is attested to by the report of curriculum changes in the 1992 *Library and Education Statistical Report*: 31 schools added new courses, 23 reviewed specific curriculum areas, 14 revised specific areas, 11 reviewed the total curriculum, and 23 taught experimental courses.[29]

Another significant area of change has been in faculty composition. The inclusion of faculty from other disciplines and without any work experience in libraries has been a noticeable trend, and the impending shortage of faculty as a result of retirements is likely to generate more change in this arena.[30] Stieg notes the increased receptivity of schools to those with non-library and information science doctorates, as well as the decline in experience requirements in faculty position descriptions. She suggests that both have been influenced by the increased emphasis on information science in the curricula of the schools. The change in experience requirements also reflects the increased emphasis on faculty research, stemming from the research emphasis of the host universities in which the schools reside.[31] Predictions are that the trend toward hiring those with Ph.D.s from outside library and information science will escalate, due to what is perceived as an insufficient supply of Ph.D.s within the discipline.[32]

Evidence of at least some positive change notwithstanding, there are ongoing calls, some in voices close to desperation, for more change, and maybe even restructuring, in graduate education for library and information science. Suggestions range from increased differentiation in education for the various possible careers and more specialization among the schools[33] to "a massive rethinking of librarianship and library and information science education" that "would lead to a major paradigm shift for the profession," presented in proposals that emphasize "feminist theories that embrace diversity, inclusiveness, connectedness, contextualization and caring...."[34] Other recommendations or predictions include the addition of undergraduate programs to the general preparation base[35] and establishment of new departments of information studies.

Implications of Change for Library and Information Science Education

The foregoing discussion has attempted to describe the societal context in which the librarians who will move into the twenty-first century will work, possible expectations of the configurations of libraries in which they will be employed, and the changing circumstances in the schools in which they will receive their initial professional preparation. Several issues remain to be addressed.

- What will these librarians need in order to be equipped for the changes that are in progress, predicted, or needed?
- How best can the LIS schools respond in providing this preparation?
- How likely is it that such preparation will be offered?

Two recent articles provide some guidance in identifying the kinds of knowledge, skills, and attitudes that will be required if librarians are to be effective in providing information services to the society of the future, regardless of what the specific structural context may be. Both stress

- competence in selection, evaluation, and application of information handling technology;

- skill in group process;
- understanding of decision making processes within the organizational bureaucracy;
- a marketing perspective: the ability to identify the information needs of those served and to design services to meet those needs; and
- understanding of the institutional and environmental context.[36]

One writer goes on to place emphasis on communication skills, stating it should be required to ensure that the value added by librarians can be articulated clearly to nonlibrarians. The overriding importance of ability to manage is also emphasized, stating in unequivocal terms that "the fundamental activity of librarianship is management."[37] Other requirements identified include an understanding of information policy issues, knowledge of the changing information infrastructure, and competency in matching the design of information products and services to the information behavior and cognitive processes of those to be served.[38]

These suggestions offer a good starting point for matching the abilities of the librarian to the likely demands of the near-term future. The current and predicted changes in libraries, including technological change and possible organizational shifts, are well addressed. Examination of the societal scenarios given above, however, suggests that there are other capabilities that will be required. Analysis of the projected changes in society suggests first of all, that librarians will need to have an increased understanding of cultural diversity and the impact of a culturally diverse population on information behavior. This need translates into a requirement for librarians who can ensure cultural diversity in information products and services and who approach information problems from the multicultural, multiethnic, multiracial, and multilingual users point of view. Such an approach requires a questioning and analytical attitude toward accepted norms and standards and a potential rethinking of the entire service structure. The transformation from a posture of making the user fit the library to one of making the library fit the user becomes even more challenging when one must discard the notion of a user with a single set of behaviors and values and move to acceptance of a mosaic of users with lifestyles, value systems, and information behavior patterns that may vary considerably from each other--and from what has been considered the norm.

This same rethinking will need to take place in regard to other demographic shifts, such as the maturing nature of the population, the increased variety in configuration of households, and the changes in the work force. The changes in family structure and in labor force composition will result in changes in information need and use patterns. The more differentiation there is within society, the less it will be possible to standardize library service and remain effective in meeting the needs of society. The individualization of information services and products is rapidly becoming technologically feasible and even affordable, but barriers continue to exist in the ways in which we conceptualize what we do.

Based on this line of thinking, one could conclude that the most critical component of the education for the librarian who will not just survive, but thrive, in the 1990s and beyond may be a reconceptualization of the role of the librarian, a new type of socialization to the profession. Some of the elements of this new orientation have already been suggested by previous writers: an emphasis on "personalized one-to-one assistance";[39] a willingness to serve as an information filter, not only to provide information but to evaluate it for the user, on the user's terms.[40] Charlie Robinson talks about the librarian as moving from being a custodian to being a navigator of knowledge, to being an information consultant.[41]

Another way in which to conceptualize this role is as an information counselor who serves in a role analogous to that of the primary health care provider, to

- diagnose the information problem;
- assess the information need;
- prescribe appropriate information products and services, or refer to specialists who can do so;
- coach effective information use and behavior;
- identify and develop needed information products and services or act as liaison with those who can;
- work to assure mechanisms for information access for those without financial resources; and
- protect information rights.

As a complement to this information counselor, another potential role is as an information systems designer who

- considers variations in the users of information systems;
- incorporates flexibility to accommodate the diversity of users;
- monitors the ways in which information needs change over time and adjusts the information system to accommodate the changes;
- studies the environment of the user and alternative information systems that may be used, so as to design for complementarity, not competition or duplication;
- accommodates differences in preference of media or format;
- adjusts the information product or service to the level of the user's need;
- allows the user to decide the appropriate degree of information filtering;
- attends to the physical, intellectual, and social accessibility of the system.

Realizations of these conceptualizations of the role of the librarian will be supported by the types of knowledge, skills, and attitudes discussed above, but will also require conscious education for change. Preparation of librarians who can deal effectively with change will need to include

- providing a sense of history and process;
- sharpening the ability to ask questions;
- fostering flexibility;
- encouraging tolerance for ambiguity;
- learning adaptation;
- inculcating freedom from ties to any particular format, technology, or institution;
- developing the ability to manage in a kaleidoscope of diversity.

Prospects

How likely is it that the current programs of library and information education will be able to provide an education that supports such a professional orientation as described above and the ability to be continuously responsive to change? One certainly cannot easily set down a list of courses that will ensure the production of individuals with such characteristics. However, there is hope to be found in the indicators mentioned earlier of changes occurring in the library and information science (LIS) schools. New courses added give indication that increased attention is being given to the individual user, the user's information behavior, and the design of interactive information products that have the capacity for individualization. Examination of new course descriptions as curriculum revision takes place suggests a trend toward deinstitutionalization of the curriculum, providing a stronger focus on basic principles that may be applied in a variety of information service settings. Such an approach moves toward freeing the student from the constraints of what is now to envision what can be–to become an agent of change.

Some of the competencies that have been identified by Malinconico and others require increased interdisciplinarity in the educational program. Areas such as cognitive psychology, organizational behavior, communication theory, and policy studies will need to be incorporated, if the schools are to be successful. The inclusion of faculty from other disciplines is helping to influence curriculum in interdisciplinary directions, not only by enabling the addition of specific courses, but also through enriching the perspective of the curriculum as a whole.

In addition, there is an institutionalized mechanism that can, if effectively used, help to provide the structure through which such changes as are needed can be implemented. The new *Standards for Accreditation of Master's Programs in Library & Information Studies 1992* embody within their statements and requirements both the seed and the process for germination of a curriculum that will prepare librarians who meet the stated characteristics and who have the capacity to serve as continuing agents of change in the provision of information service. The *Standards* specifically call for a curriculum that

- fosters development of library and information professionals who will assume an assertive role in providing services
- emphasizes an evolving body of knowledge that reflects the findings of basic and applied research from relevant fields
- integrates the theory, application, and use of technology
- responds to the needs of a rapidly changing multicultural, multiethnic, multilingual society including the needs of underserved groups

- responds to the needs of a rapidly changing technological and global society
- provides direction for future development of the field
- promotes commitment to continuous professional growth.[42]

Just as important, the *Standards* require a process of continual curriculum review and evaluation and the use of such assessment in planning for ongoing improvement and change.[43] The themes of responsiveness, evaluation, and change are pervasive throughout the *Standards*. If these themes are infused into the tenor of the programs that the *Standards* were written to assist, there is hope that the kinds of education needed to prepare individuals to serve and to lead in a time of change will be forthcoming.

For the schools of library and information science, the balance among responsiveness to the immediate demands of the profession, the expectations of the university, and the future needs of the students requires in many regards the same type of flexibility, adaptability, tolerance for ambiguity, and management within a kaleidoscope of diversity that have been suggested as hallmarks of what is required for the librarians of the future. If these characteristics can be modeled within the schools, there is a strong chance that such characteristics will be developed within their students.

Just as libraries are creatures of the society they serve and must be both responsive to change and proactive in bringing about change if they are to survive, the LIS schools must be responsive to the needs of the profession for which students are being educated. The schools will both initiate and respond to the changes in the profession and in society—or they too will be replaced. Although some may prefer this approach, evolutionary change within the schools can make such action unnecessary.

NOTES

1. Computed from U.S. Bureau of the Census, *Statistical Abstract of the United States: 1991* (Washington: U.S. Government Printing Office, 1991), Table 15, 14 and Table 17, 15.

2. Population Research Unit, Department of Finance, [State of California], "Projected Total Population for California by Race/Ethnicity, July 1, 1970 to July 1, 2020," Report 88 P-4, February 1988 (mimeographed), [2].

3. Joseph F. Coates, Jennifer Jarratt, and John B. Mahaffie, "Future Work," *The Futurist* 25 (May-June 1991): 10.

4. Ibid.

5. Computed from U.S. Bureau of the Census, *Statistical Abstract of the United States: 1991*, Table 18, 16.

6. Computed from U.S. Bureau of the Census, *Statistical Abstract of the United States: 1991*, Table 57, 45.

7. United Way Strategic Institute, "Nine Forces Reshaping America," *The Futurist* 24 (July-August 1990): 15. The projection is based on growth from 1988 to 2000.

8. "Measures of Change," *U.S. News & World Report*, 25 December 1989/1 January 1990, 66; Marvin J. Cetron and Margaret Evans Gayle, "Educational Renaissance: 43 Trends for U.S. Schools," *The Futurist* 24 (September-October 1990): 39.

9. Coates, Jarratt, and Mahaffie, 11-13, 15; "Measures of Change," 66; United Way Strategic Institute, 11; Cetron and Gayle, 34.

10. Coates, Jarratt, and Mahaffie, 12-13; Julie L. Nicklin, "Helping to Manage Diversity in the Work Force," *The Chronicle of Higher Education*, 30 September 1992, A5.

11. United Way Strategic Institute, 12; Cetron and Gayle, 37.

12. United Way Strategic Institute, 10.

13. Computed from U.S. Bureau of the Census, *Statistical Abstract of the United States: 1991*, Table 215, 132.

14. Ibid., and Table 232, 143.

15. Charles G. Treadwell, "Demographic Changes and Higher Education," *The Education Digest* 57 (February 1992), 33-34.

16. Cetron and Gayle, 36.

17. "Mass. Town Loses Library Service After Nixing Tax Cap Override," "LAPL Cuts Hours and Books," "Phoenix PL Staff Furlough Themselves," and "Drastic Cuts in Fairfax County" all appeared in *American Libraries* 23 (September 1992): 614, 617-18, 624, 720. Also see "California County Libs. Chafe Awaiting Budget Cuts," *Library Journal* 117 (September 15, 1992): 12-13; "Illinois Budget Hurts Regional Libs.," *Library Journal* 117 (September 1, 1992): 112.

18. See, for example, Anne Woodsworth and others, "The Model Research Library: Planning for the Future," *Journal of Academic Librarianship* 15 (July 1989): 132-38; Jordan M. Scepanski, "Library 1995," *Library Administration & Management* 2 (Spring 1990): 74-76; Anne Lipow, "21st Century Library Position Announcement," Visions Listserv, August 7, 1992 (alipow@library Berkeley. EDU).

19. S. Michael Malinconico, "What Librarians Need to Know to Survive in an Age of Technology," *Journal of Education for Library and Information Science* 33 (Summer 1992): 226-27, 232-33.

20. John A. McCrossan, "Public Library Directors' Opinion About Future Directions for Library Services, *Public Library Quarterly* 11, no. 3 (1991): 5-17.

21. For example, a viewpoint expressed in the program "Views from Across the Quad: The University's Expectations for the Library of the 21st Century" presented at the American Library Association 1992 Annual Conference, June 27, 1992, San Francisco, by David Riggs, Stanford University Professor of English, was that librarians should not be responsible for implementing technology.

22. Fourteen have closed since 1978; one more is scheduled to close in 1993.

23. Marion Paris, "Library School Closings: The Need for Action," *Library Quarterly* 61 (July 1991): 260-61.

24. See, for example, "Perspectives on the Elimination of Graduate Programs in Library and Information Studies: A Symposium," *Library Quarterly* 61 (July 1991): 259-93; Marion Paris, "Why Library Schools Fail," *Library Journal* 115 (October 1, 1990): 38-42; Marion Paris, "The Dilemma of Library School Closings, *Libraries and Information Services Today* (Chicago: American Library Association, 1991), 23-27; and Jonathan R. Cole, *Report of the Provost on the School of Library Service at Columbia University* (April 13, 1990).

25. See, for example, C. D. Hurt, "The Future of Library Science in Higher Education: A Crossroads for Library Science and Librarianship," *Advances in Librarianship* (New York :Academic Press, 1992 in press), 47 in manuscript copy.

26. Association for Library and Information Science Education, *Library and Information Science Education Statistical Report 1992*, ed. Timothy W. Sineath (Raleigh, NC: ALISE, 1992), 297, 300.

27. Ibid., 296-97.

28. Margaret Stieg in *Change and Challenge in Library Education* (Chicago: American Library Association, 1992) notes that the area in which there has been the most curricula change in the previous ten years has been in addition of new courses in technology and information science (112).

29. Association for Library and Information Science Education, 317.

30. The shortage of qualified faculty for schools of library and information studies (LIS schools) has been a matter of concern over the last several years. The recent study by Futas and Zipkowitz indicates that the situation is worsening (Elizabeth Futas and Fay Zipkowitz, "The Faculty Vanishes," *Library Journal* 116 [September 1, 1991]: 148-52).

31. Stieg, 84-87.

32. Hurt, 49.

33. Stieg, 176-77.

34. Jane Anne Hannigan, "Project Century 21: A Report," Working Paper prepared for American Library Association President's Committee for Project Century 21, June 1992, 1.

35. Hurt, 42-43, 47-48.

36. Malinconico, 233-39; Anne Woodsworth and June Lester, "Educational Imperatives of the Future Research Library," *Journal of Academic Librarianship* 17 (September 1991): 207-8.

37. Malinconico, 238.

38. Woodsworth and Lester, 207-8.

39. Herbert S. White, "Libraries and Librarians in the Next Millennium," *Library Journal* 115 (May 15, 1990): 55.

40. Bernard Vavrek, "The Future of Public Libraries, Extension of Remarks," *Wilson Library Bulletin* (May 1991): 26; Woodsworth and Lester, 207.

41. Charles Robinson, "The Public Library Vanishes," *Library Journal* 117 (March 15, 1992): 54.

42. *Standard for Accreditation of Master's Programs in Library and Information Studies, 1992* (Chicago: Office for Accreditation, American Library Association, 1992): 11-12.

43. Ibid., 12.

The Time for Transformational Leadership Is Now!

Donald E. Riggs
Vivian M. Sykes

INTRODUCTION

Libraries are currently undergoing the greatest degree of change in their history. This change is driven by several factors. Technology, for example, is making it possible to provide more value-added services for library users. Online public access catalogs enable users to have bibliographic access to nearly all of the library's holdings, while the card catalog permitted access to only about 60 percent of a library's bibliographic records. The OPAC also allows commercial and locally-produced databases to be accessed from remote areas outside of the library. Access to other libraries' OPACs is now available via Internet. The virtual library, in a sense, is already a reality. Expert systems and even principles of neural networking are being used to improve users' services. More electronic full texts are available for libraries. Some libraries are creating online textual analysis projects whereby scholars can do the work that formerly required 16 years in only 16 seconds. The larger virtues of technology are yet to come to libraries.

Donald E. Riggs is Dean of the University Library and Professor of Information and Library Studies, University of Michigan, Ann Arbor, MI. Vivian M. Sykes is a doctoral student in the School of Information and Library Studies at the University of Michigan.

[Haworth co-indexing entry note]: "The Time for Transformational Leadership Is Now!" Riggs, Donald E. and Vivian M. Sykes. Co-published simultaneously in the *Journal of Library Administration* (The Haworth Press, Inc.) Vol. 18, No. 3/4, 1993, pp. 55-68; and: *Catalysts for Change: Managing Libraries in the 1990s* (ed: Gisela M. von Dran and Jennifer Cargill) The Haworth Press, Inc., 1993, pp. 55-68. Multiple copies of this article/chapter may be purchased from The Haworth Document Delivery Center [1-800-3-HAWORTH; 9:00 a.m. - 5:00 p.m. (EST)].

The workplace is now more diverse than ever in libraries. And, sadly to say, libraries in general have only done a fraction of the work that needs to be done in building and improving diversity in their staff, collections, and services. Greater emphasis is required in recruiting people of color. Librarians should begin working with elementary and secondary school children of color in persuading them to choose librarianship for their professional career. And it is obvious that each library has to do a better job in fostering a work environment that encourages members of a diverse staff to remain with the respective library. Parts of the diversity locus are missing when libraries ignore the collections and services. Both of these important areas must reflect a commitment of the library leadership toward diversity.

The library staff is being asked to do more with less. A "revenue diet" in libraries has created staff reductions at the same time when users' expectations are at an all time high. The more value-added services given to users, the more they expect. Staff members are working under uncommon stress while concurrently the library's parent organization cannot provide relief in the way of additional staff support. The new technology has brought forth necessary additional staff training. As the result of implementing new technology, new roles for the staff are being created without funds for the much-needed training.

Skyrocketing annual increases in certain journal subscriptions are playing havoc with the acquisitions budget. The day may be over when each major research library can have its own "crown jewels" in respective collections. We are already witnessing more cooperation among all sizes and types of libraries. Developing collections on the premise that "just in case" users may want specific items is indeed being challenged by the "just in time" concept of borrowing the item from another library or acquiring it from a commercial vendor. More funds are being reallocated to resource sharing, and we can expect this trend to continue. The traditional practice of building paper collections is already under scrutiny in some libraries. Publishers are beginning to better understand the financial plight of libraries.

The foregoing changes in libraries are just a few samples of the modifications and new directions being thrust upon libraries. It is obvious that a new type of library leadership is required to capture and reformulate the opportunities offered by these changing times.

MANAGERS AND LEADERS

First, it is important to emphasize that both managers and leaders are necessary in order to have an efficient and effective library. Managers tend to focus on the efficiency aspects of a library and leaders improve its effectiveness. Leaders are more deeply involved with the overall direction of the library. Managers are more internally focused, paying attention to the day-to-day activities. Managers do things right; leaders do the right things. Interests of library leaders transcend organizational boundaries including external constituencies. While the manager is solving problems, the leader is setting the agenda. It is very important for the leader to think about the library's future and to invent ways to make the desired future happen. Library leaders have to be vitally interested in the aspirations and expectations of their followers and work with them in translating jointly-held intentions into reality.

THE CASE FOR TRANSFORMATIONAL LEADERSHIP

The transformational leader can be expected to move the library from its current situation to a new future, create visions of potential opportunities, instill new cultures and strategies, and mobilize the energy and resources of the staff toward concerted goals and objectives. Transforming leaders like to make things happen. They motivate the library staff to do more than is necessary. Under their leadership, they infuse new values in the library. They make followers feel good about themselves. Transformational leaders support the deepest psychological needs of followers; people want to feel they are doing a good job and want recognition for it. These leaders follow the basic dictum of a West Pointer: "Make sure your troops are settled and fed before you take care of your own needs."

Unquestionably, libraries are undergoing dramatic changes. These changes required forward-thinking, humanistic leaders who will ask the right questions, challenge the mission of the library, and move beyond the status quo. In short, as libraries change, their directors, assistant directors, and in some instances department heads have to possess and exercise the attributes of transformational leaders.

Transformational library leaders cannot see around corners, but they must be able to hold a vision and formulate goals, objectives, and strategies for realizing that vision. What will the library be like 10 years hence? It is difficult for anyone to accurately prognosticate what the library will be a decade from now. Nevertheless, someone has to be visualizing the future of the library and designing pathways to reach the desired future.

Transformational leaders are likely to generate the images of the future and then sort them into three piles. First, the "possible future" will be the largest pile and it will evolve from the present conditions of the library. Second, the "probable future" will be supported by evidence strong enough to establish presumptions but not based on actual proof. This pile is a subset of the "possible future." And the last pile is known as the "preferable future." Essentially, this pile is the one the transforming leader will find most exciting since it will lead to desirable outcomes of the library.

A futures-creative leader is literally a designer of the future. Walt Disney redesigned the amusement park. Martin Luther King, Jr. rekindled the civil rights movement. Dr. King was most certainly a visionary and is well remembered for his "I have a dream" statement. Betty Friedan reconceptualized the role of women in America. Napoleon was an early pioneer of futures-creative leadership. He rose to a leadership position in a time of great change and turmoil. His foresight generally enabled him to be prepared for setbacks. He had the ability to anticipate in a manner that little took him by surprise. Futures-creative library leaders must be able to deal with three or four alternatives at the same time. Their visionary role encompasses a combination of idealism and realism.

Strategic Planning

Creating the library's future will not occur simply as happenstance. A carefully-crafted strategic plan is necessary if the library's future is going to unfold in a systematic manner. Strategic planning is a process involving the entire library staff, and it is a process that is never completed and is periodically being refined and updated. The plan itself should be perceived as "organic" in the sense that it is a "live" working document that is under continual review.

The transformational leader will undoubtedly find the strategic plan of great value in communicating the future direction of the library. After an environmental scan is done of the current internal and external factors impacting the library, a self-analysis of the library is encouraged. These types of activities can be coordinated by a Strategic Planning Committee; this group should consist of representatives throughout the library. The library director, who is the library's chief strategist, should chair the committee. After relevant information on the current status of the library is obtained, the committee should draft a vision statement for the library. This statement could provide an overview of what the library will be like and how it will change 10 years hence. There is not anything magical about 10 years; however, any projections beyond a decade will probably not reflect reality. Following review of the mission statement by the entire library staff and appropriate other people, the committee drafts a mission statement. A broad, philosophical "umbrella" statement is the best way to describe the mission statement. It describes what the library is now doing and wants to do in the future. The draft mission statement should be shared with the entire library staff and their recommendations for improving it should be encouraged.

The vision and mission statements are followed by a draft of the goals for the library. Again, after the committee has drafted the goals; the entire library should have an opportunity to review them and offer revisions. Goals are broad, encompassing statements that point the library in the direction of what it wants to become. They should be long-range and must be revisited at least annually for updating, revising, and replacing after achieved.

After the first renditions of the vision and mission statements and the goals have been discussed and agreed on, the prudent transformational leader may want to hold a retreat for the library administrators (including all department heads) to discuss objectives and strategies for each goal. Objectives are more specific than goals; they are quantifiable and can be measured. The essence of strategic planning is strategy. A strategy is a course of action for achieving goals and objectives. Without strategies, the library is like a ship without a rudder. Library leaders cannot abdicate their responsibility in the creation of strategies. Installing purpose in lieu of improvisation, and planned progress in place of organization drift are, first and foremost, the responsibilities of the library director. As in any organization, the library director cannot, and should not be expected to do all of the planning. Thus, the role of the Strategic Planning Committee is substantiated. One of the functions of dynamic leadership is to ensure that the library's strategies possess a magnetic and cohesive quality. The formulation of strategies cannot be done in a vacuum. After the draft strategies are created, they must be shared freely within the library for constructive refinement. The director's advisory board should have a chance to provide their comments to the improvement of the strategies and eventually the entire plan. To remain functional, strategies should be evaluated annually to see if they are still timely, consistent, achievable, explicit enough, and legal. After sufficient time, a strategy may run its course and needs to be replaced. Strategies may be merged with other strategies, sub-strategies or co-strategies may be developed.

As the library transforms, its strategic plan has to be evaluated at least annually to see if it is still on track toward the realization of goals and objectives. Questions like "What went right?" and "What went wrong?" are good starters in assessing the plan. Libraries experienced in strategic planning have learned that the process of strategic planning may be of as much benefit as the actual plan itself. The process permits an unusual opportunity to look at the entire library fabric, and to pinpoint its strengths and weaknesses. Such opportunities are of prime importance during the turbulent, ever-changing times currently taking place in libraries.

Creativity

Based on the dictionary's definition, "creativity" is the act of making or producing and, more specifically, the act of making something new. With this definition in mind, pure mental activity without a resulting product is not creativity. This distinction is important, because people often assume that thought is in itself creative and are willing to pay large sums of money for think tanks from which the product is often minimal. True creativity is invention, or the process of making something new. Creativity is the combining of disconnected, apparently unrelated elements in a unique way to provide something useful. The more remotely the elements of the new combination, the more creative the process or solution. Creative library staff practice "divergent thinking"–the kind of thinking that is constantly attuned to new possibilities.

Creativity is a neglected topic in librarianship. Few schools of information and library studies accredited by the American Library Association promote the study of creativity. Practicing librarians get bogged down with their daily work duties and they forget and/or choose not to think beyond the comforts of routine tasks. It is left to the creative librarian to transcend these familiar activities and think of alternative methods for handling a problem or perhaps changing a situation. Few libraries reward their library staff for creative activities. Deterrents to creativity in libraries include: (1) Pressure to conform; (2) fear of failure; (3) natural resistance to change; (4) lack of confidence; (5) laziness; (6) fear of ridicule; (7) habit; (8) pessimism; and (9) timidity.

Following are some expressions heard in libraries that restrict creativity:

1. It won't work in our library.
2. We tried similar ideas before.
3. The budget won't allow it.
4. Why change it? It's still working ok.
5. It's not practical for our type of library.
6. Our library is too small for it.
7. Nobody ever did it before.
8. Let's get back to reality.
9. Let's have a committee evaluate it.

Nearly everyone is born with a degree of creativity. It has been known for generations that creativity can be taught. As a person becomes enculturated, creativity may be lost or inhibited. The school system in America tends to pose an end to creativity. Children up until the age of nine are generally very creative. Rules, regulations, and the requirement to conform inhibits creativity in young people.

The two hemispheres (right and left sides) of the human brain are getting more attention in the different roles they play in creativity. The left hemisphere is considered the dominant side of the brain, while the right hemisphere is used significantly less. If we are to increase our capacity for creativity, the right side of the brain has to be developed; this side of the brain works in contrast to the action of the left brain and its development is frequently neglected in our formal education. Bry believes that:

> Without the full use of our "right brain," we are at best using only half of our potential, like those who have favored one foot over another, we have wound up limping and lopsided. But that part of us is always accessible, if only we choose to reach inward to it. Once we have rediscovered it, we can then allow it to work cooperatively with the more highly developed "left-brain."[1]

Libraries are staffed with many talented individuals. How can library leaders enhance opportunities for these people to use their latent creative abilities? This is one of the major challenges facing library leadership, and it becomes greater as libraries continue to change at a significant speed.

Innovation by Substitution

Innovation follows creativity in the sense that the development of new products/services come after the idea. Generally, innovation is well planned with a purpose. It is based on what the library "should be doing." Three kinds of innovation occurs in libraries: (1) innovation in service, (2) innovation in products, and (3) innovation in management.

The traditional library emphasizes "more and better" and the innovative library advocates "new and different." Faced with financial constraints, innovative libraries are finding it difficult to begin new services, for example, without some "seed" money. How do libraries overcome this serious obstacle? Transformational leaders will take the initiative to see if an existing service can be abandoned or modified in order to have resources to sponsor the new service. "Innovation by substitution" has to be handled judiciously to prevent staff morale issues. Relocating staff members from an established service to a new and different service has to be done thoughtfully and not simply for the sake of doing something new. The establishment of criteria or a model for "innovating by substituting" would serve the library well in better understanding the rationale for such an approach. Purposeful innovation can return many dividends to the library.

Intrapreneurs

According to Pinchot, innovation almost never happens in large organizations without an individual or small group passionately dedicated to making it happen. When such people start up new companies, they are called entrepreneurs. Inside organizations we call them intrapreneurs.[2] Libraries are in dire need of more intrapreneurs, since so few of them can be found. Intrapreneurs are described as rugged individualists who have difficulty working within the boundaries of bureaucracies. They are dedicated and "self driven" to resolve a problem, improve a service, or create a new product or service. They may rub people the wrong way because of their low level of tolerance for indecision, unproductive committees, and participatory management techniques. These are people who know what they want to do and what it takes to make their dream a reality. They are not necessarily good team players and do not appreciate being asked to conform to established policies and practices. In a nutshell, they may be perceived as "wild ducks" in the library and may even be difficult to manage.

Even though intrapreneurs may upset the equilibrium of a library, transformational leaders will undoubtedly recognize their value and make arrangements to give them proper latitude to achieve focused goals and objectives. As technology is becoming more specialized in application, intrapreneurship will be required to create more value-added services. The leadership of the library should run the risk of employing intrapreneurs who have the brilliance and dedication to make major breakthroughs in library technology. More of these trail blazers are needed in today's libraries. The trick is to balance individual efforts of the intrapreneurs with the slow-moving, traditional bureaucratic structure.

Gender Differences

Judy Rosener sparked some controversy in her *Harvard Business Review* article on the leadership style of women. She believes that women leaders have broken the glass ceiling in organizations and that effective leaders do not come from one mold.[3] Unquestionably, there are inherent differences in the interactions of men and women leaders. On the other hand, there are many similarities. In her study in which she asked men and women executives to describe their leadership styles, Rosener found that:

> The similarities end when men and women leaders describe their leadership performance and how they usually influence those with whom they work. The men are more likely to describe themselves in ways that characterize the command-and-control leadership style. They view job performance as a series of transactions with subordinates ... they are more likely to use power that comes from their place in the organization. The women respondents, on the other hand, described themselves as getting subordinates to transform their own self-interest into the interests of the group through concern for a broader goal. ... More specifically, the women encourage participation, share power, and enhance other people's self-worth.[4]

In a later issue of the *Harvard Business Review*, Cynthia Epstein debates Rosener's findings. She believes Rosener's mode of investigation is impaired to begin with; instead of observing men and women at work to ascertain whether they indeed act differently, Rosener asked them to describe their differences.[5] Much current research reveals that men and women tend to stereotype their own behavior according to cultural views of gender-appropriate behavior. It is time to reconsider the excessive and inappropriate sex typing that takes place, whether offered in the service of improving women's situations or restricting them. Women ought to be in management because they are intelligent, adaptable, practical, and efficient–and because they are capable of compassion, as are men.[6]

The transforming library needs both the female and male experience. For too long, differential treatment in the library workplace has been based on the assumption that women are more receptive to and comfortable with repetitious work and are reluctant to engage in adversarial activities. This has not turned out to be true. Perhaps it is time to stop talking about the gender differences and get on with the job of providing dynamic leadership for our libraries, regardless of gender. The category we should be focusing on is "people," not men and women.

Changing Metaphors

Gardening is an excellent metaphor for achieving change in libraries. Transforming and encouraging plants require hard work, patience, and a great deal of cultivation. The correct culture or soil for plants is very important to their growth and development. Some parts of the garden require shade while others have to enjoy the benefit of full sun. Many of the plants contribute to the garden's raison d'etre and leave after the first frost. And there are the perennials which seem to hold the garden together.

The work of a library leader is very much like that of a gardener. Each library leader should have a working metaphor for describing how to create and implement change. Problem solving, visualizing, and coping with disappointment can all be experienced through gardening. Ongoing changes in the garden are brought about by drought, too much rain, frost, insects, and competitors (the weeds). Even though the changes are not necessarily brought forth by the same reasons in the library, they are similar enough to make the analogy. Each library can be seen as a garden or a series of several gardens. Each staff member is a special being requiring its own special culture for growing and succeeding. And each person can be seen as contributing, in a special way, to a multi-dimensional garden mosaic.

Risk Taking

Traditionally, libraries do not encourage risk taking. There are many reasons for such an attitude, including insufficient funds for experimentation and a strong commitment to providing reliable core services. Resources will chiefly determine the level of risk that can be taken. Timing is of utmost importance in risk taking. King and Cleland note that the interrelationship of timing and risk is an important matter in strategic allocation decisions, as illustrated through questions such as: (1) Should we undertake this strategic project now or delay it until the situation becomes more clear (and less risky)? and (2) would a commitment of resources now be warranted on the grounds that this activity will itself resolve the uncertainty?[7]

The library director must take the lead in providing resources and encouragement for calculated risk taking. Special funding such as getting a private donor to establish a fund for risk taking may have to be put in place before any substantive movement can be made in this area. A "venture capital" account for risk taking will eventually prove to be a good investment. Intrapreneurs, for example, will require some "seed" money for equipment or human resources.

As important as the funding for the risk taking endeavor is the director's attitude and commitment. Allowing latitude in the library's organizational construct for making mistakes is mandatory if staff members are going to feel comfortable while engaging in risky ventures. If library leaders are genuinely interested in creating new services and products for their users, then they must "walk the talk" of risk taking. The fear of failure has to be removed from the library; the person responsible for removing this fear is the director. A certain number of errors will be inevitable in any risk-taking endeavor. Embarrassment and the "guilty" feeling associated with failure have to be eradicated; they must be replaced with encouragement and understanding. Creativity and intrapreneurship cannot be fostered in an "anti-risk-taking" environment. Holding workshops on the value of risk taking, and its crucial interrelationships with creativity and intrapreneurship, would serve as encouragement for the staff to participate in risk-taking endeavors. The director and assistant directors must take a sincere interest in each staff member's risk-taking project. Mutual trust is engendered from this personal interest in the respective project. The workplace encouraging risk taking also has to be a nonthreatening environment.

Should libraries be on the leading edge or on the trailing edge? It is assumed that, if money was not an issue, most libraries would choose to be a leader rather than a follower. However, it is interesting to note that very few journal articles and books are written on library leadership. Moreover, most libraries "innovate" by replicating the work of others. In essence, library leaders have to be greater risk takers themselves, and enhance the opportunities for their staff to experiment with, create, and implement new products/services.

Communication

The vast changes in libraries bring a greater need to communicate more extensively with the entire library staff. Along with the unknown comes fear and apprehension about how changes will impact the work lives of the staff. Communication has to be upward, downward, and lateral in order to communicate effectively with the entire staff. Nothing should be taken for granted in communication. Minutes of the library's top decision making body should be carried in the library-wide newsletter. Electronic mail should be used when appropriate. Library-wide meetings should be held occasionally to bring the staff up to date on new endeavors, planning activities, major changes, and the financial situation.

Transformational leadership should illustrate via various communiques how new values are being infused in the library, how creativity and intrapreneurship are being encouraged, and how the vision and mission statements are being translated into reality. The well-worn phrase "you can never over communicate" is more relevant today in our changing libraries than ever before; it contains a straight-forward message for library leaders about the urgency to improve their communication practices.

CONCLUSION

Now is the most exciting time in our civilization to work in libraries. Associated with this excitement, we find turbulence, apprehension, stressful working conditions, insufficient budgets, and ever-changing libraries. New management techniques do not offer a quick fix or instant gratification. There are no "one-minute managers" in today's library world. Changes occurring in libraries are fast and robust. Libraries are getting poised to make a quantum leap into the future.

Transformational leadership is required now for our libraries. We cannot wait for this type of leadership to gradually evolve. Libraries have to be lead by individuals who can (with the participation of their staff) plan effectively and realize goals and objectives that significantly improve services for their respective users. Transformational leaders are "people persons" who understand human motives, aspirations, and the need for self-actualization. They are also individuals who can create and articulate a vision for their libraries. They know how to strengthen their followers and possess a gift for institution building. The transformation leader creates a legacy that will last a long time.

Some of the transformation of a library comes about in a subtle manner. Even though changes may be fast, their impact on the library's culture may not be noticed immediately. The concept of transforming leadership carries with it an implicit endorsement of renewal–a needed ingredient in libraries today. In closing, it is appropriate to relate an Hungarian folktale that tells of a wise man walking down a country road with a group of students.

> "Look at that tree full of birds," he said as he threw a rock to roust the flock. "Now look again," he said after the birds settled back in the branches. "That's how the world changes." "But we don't understand," his students demanded. "All the birds are back." "Ah," said the old man with a knowing smile, "but each bird is sitting on a different branch." (Author unknown)

NOTES

1. Adelaide Bry, *Directing the Movies of Your Mind: Visualization for Health and Insight.* (New York: Harper & Row, 1978), p. 12.

2. Gifford Pinchot, *Intrapreneuring: You Don't Have to Leave the Corporation to Become an Entrepreneur.* (New York: Harper & Row, 1985), p. 6.

3. Judy B. Rosener, "Ways Women Lead," *Harvard Business Review* 68 (November-December 1990): 119-125.

4. Ibid., p. 120.

5. Cynthia F. Epstein, "Ways Men and Women Lead," *Harvard Business Review* 69 (January-February 1991): 150-160.

6. Ibid., p. 151.

7. William R. King and David I. Cleland, *Strategic Planning and Policy.* (New York: Van Nostrand Reinhold, 1978), p. 213.

Managing the Academic Library Through Teamwork: A Case Study

Susan P. Besemer
Sarah B. Dorsey
Barbara L. Kittle
Carrie M. Niles

If necessity is the mother of Invention, then perhaps desperation might be Inspiration's father. How many useful innovations that seem to others like bright and shiny new ideas are created as the result of a last-ditch attempt to fix a part of the world that had just been noticed to be "out of order?" Perhaps that is not a very romantic view of change, but it often fits experience. And if a new idea works, by bringing about needed improvements, it looks better and better.

In earlier decades, the gradual pace of change led managers to believe that they could cope with reversals by merely modifying and fine-tuning their organizations. But lately in many enterprises, and very recently in libraries, changes have come about so quickly that mere tinkering won't solve the problems.

Susan P. Besemer is Director of Library Services, Daniel A. Reed Library; Sarah B. Dorsey is Senior Assistant Librarian (Music Librarian); Barbara L. Kittle is Associate Librarian (Reference); and Carrie M. Niles is Senior Assistant Librarian (Head of Bibliographic Control) All are at SUNY College, Fredonia, NY.

[Haworth co-indexing entry note]: "Managing the Academic Library Through Teamwork: A Case Study." Besemer, Susan P., Sarah B. Dorsey, Barbara L. Kittle and Carrie M. Niles. Co-published simultaneously in the *Journal of Library Administration* (The Haworth Press, Inc.) Vol. 18, No. 3/4, 1993, pp. 69-89; and: *Catalysts for Change: Managing Libraries in the 1990s* (ed: Gisela M. von Dran and Jennifer Cargill) The Haworth Press, Inc., 1993, pp. 69-89. Multiple copies of this article/chapter may be purchased from The Haworth Document Delivery Center [1-800-3-HAWORTH; 9:00 a.m. - 5:00 p.m. (EST)].

© 1993 by The Haworth Press, Inc. All rights reserved.

In organizations where environmental change has disrupted and sometimes overturned the status quo, some managers have used the energy generated by these dislocations as catalysts to forge stronger entities, to pursue new directions, and to leapfrog over old ideas that no longer work to lay new plans that just may work better.

W. Edwards Deming published a book in 1986 which was to become a handbook or manual for change in organizations inspired by his leadership. *Out of the Crisis* described Deming's method for saving American businesses through a transformation of management that included the use of work groups or teams. These work groups did problem-solving on topics close to their interests, improving quality in manufacturing and in service industries.[1]

Crisis can be the catalyst that forces a transformation. Managers who are achieving expected levels of productivity and meeting their goals and those of others have no need for changing the status quo. When sudden changes in the environment rock the foundations of the organization, looking for new ways to cope often occurs just one step before panic.

The literature of management has discussed the use of teams in organizations since the 1960s,[2] with many important books appearing in the 1970s and 1980s.[3] Several articles with a team "flavor" appeared in the library literature early in the 1980s giving encouragement to the idea of "collegial management."[4-6] The concept was worked out in a practical sense at Dickinson College, where earlier goals of mere "participative management" were overturned by a new shared management concept. This structural reorganization was stimulated by the search by the librarians at Dickinson for a new and appropriate librarian status, distinct from that of administration or faculty.

The literature of librarianship slowly began to reflect interest in team organization in the middle to late 1980s.[7-10] It was not until library managers recognized that they simply couldn't cope with present and emerging problems under the then-existing traditional organizational framework that they began to question the basic premise of the organizational structure of the academic library. Excellent articles discussing the theory and practice of team management in libraries have been seen more frequently since 1990.[11,12]

A CHANGING ENVIRONMENT

What were some of the issues that began shocking academic libraries in the mid-1980s that continue to confound us today? Let's start by considering changes in the external environment. Lower levels of budgetary support for higher education by government, combined with sky-rocketing inflation in the serials publishing industry were changing the character of our collections, while we stood by and helplessly watched our ability to buy an adequate number of monographs dwindle. The value of the dollar on the world market further complicated our love-hate relationship with already-costly serials published abroad. Automation was an accomplished goal for large libraries, but some managers were unhappy with the quality and level of access that early systems provided, and were looking forward to migrating to more powerful and flexible user-friendly applications. Meanwhile, small and mid-sized libraries were still trying to plot a course toward their first automated systems. Students began to be more assertive in their demands for improved services, and faculty were outspoken about their needs from the library, pushed by increased institutional pressure to perform and publish research.

The internal environment of the academic library was also stressed by change. The hierarchical and bureaucratic library organization was a maze which library users had to navigate to get the services they needed. Sometimes library faculty and staff were stuck in positions with job descriptions written eons ago, while the need for additional staff to attend to tasks emerging from technological changes went unmet because of static or reduced budgets. Middle-level managers, the heads of divisions, were sometimes relegated to bureaucratic tasks that challenged only their tolerance for boredom, while other librarians might sit in positions for twenty years with no clear career path to promotion or to upward and outward mobility. Staff patterns were sometimes rigid, with areas assuming petty territorialities which related neither to need nor logic, but only to history and ego. Add to the mix the changed expectations of staff brought about by technology. Who really knows enough to transform our services to deal effectively with the complex universe of information that libraries must master now and in the future?

The true and simple answer to this question is to say that we do. Collectively, we know or can learn everything we need to know, although individually we may have areas of weakness as well as strength. The only truly unlimited resource in this challenging world is our talent, for that grows to meet opportunity and expands exponentially when nurtured by a supportive work environment.

FREDONIA'S EXPERIMENT

Pushed by the external environment and shoved by the internal one, we at the SUNY College at Fredonia's Reed Library embarked early in 1987 on a planning and problem-solving process that would result in pursuing an experimental new pathway. Our staff of fewer than thirty persons felt the environmental pressures acutely. These were most often experienced as a need for additional staff members to take on new technology-related tasks. But the fiscal climate did not encourage optimism for new personnel lines. Like other organizations that experienced pressure to change, we looked upon our situation as not altogether discouraging, but as an opportunity to try something new. Other libraries were confronting similar situations,[13] but we did not know that team experiments were also beginning in other institutions.

With two retirements of senior librarians, we at Reed Library seized an opportunity to reshape, and perhaps transform, our environment to make it a more effective agent for service and to allow it to be more supportive of our individual and collective professional and personal growth. We began with a task force to consider the issue and ended with a new management structure built around two teams of library faculty and staff.

Is our structure new? It depends on who is asked that question. Does it work? We think so, but whether or not it works better than a traditional structure is not easy to say. Some evidence will be presented later that suggests that it is working well. Our experiment will conclude in another year, and we'll decide then what we want to do next. In the following pages we'll describe our structure and share how it feels to work in the team environment. (See Appendix A for Reed Library's Team Structure at a Glance.) Our authors are all practicing librarians at Reed Library, using the team structure to get the job done. We do not see everything the same way, but we all share a commitment, for now at least, to making the system work for us and for the best service of our clientele.

How can we describe the structure? Although it can be diagramed, our structure looks more like the inter-linking loops of a bangle necklace than the stepladder of a traditional library, since so much of our work takes place working in small groups with interlocking relationships with other groups.

A TEAM STRUCTURE

The real work of the Library takes place at service points including those in Technical Services. In these units, library faculty and staff meet regularly to discuss work flow, problems, new ideas, and to encourage one another. The librarian in charge of each area then takes the issues emerging from her or his area to the weekly Team Meeting for either the Technical Services Team or the Public Access Team. Each team is composed of five or six librarians and the Library Clerk III from the clerical support staff of either Technical Services or Public Access. At the team level, ideas are discussed, debated, and policy recommendations are brought forth from the team. The Team Leaders (appointed by the Director for two-year nonrenewable terms) then meet weekly with the Director to discuss news, problems, and solutions coming from the teams. Minutes of these meetings are kept and distributed as soon as possible to all staff members. The Director uses this weekly meeting to report to Library staff information which she has gathered from meetings with the College administration, problems that have surfaced from patrons, and ideas that she has had or that others have shared. The occasional policy change is a decision made at these meetings by consensus among the Team Leaders and the Director. Most meetings are information sharing and problem solving sessions, as are those at the unit level.

Team Leaders play a critical role in the organization. They are practicing librarians who take on administrative duties as an overload, and for a stipend equivalent to that given to academic department chairs. Assuming this challenging role provides professional development and learning experiences unlike those available in any other way. One of our authors will comment on her experience as a

Team Leader for a two-year term. The position may be likened to that of a Head of Technical Services, or Head of Readers' Services, but it is not a "life sentence" as is the more traditional position. All Team Leaders to date have been eager to shed the mantle of team leadership at the end of their terms, but it is possible that this experience could encourage a budding manager to envision himself or herself as a director or another administrator. At the very least, former Team Leaders have become much more sensitive to the exigencies of library management, and have become more understanding both of the Director and of colleagues on their own and on the other team.

CARRIE NILES: A TEAM LEADER'S VIEW

"One of the biggest challenges leaders face today is translating their vision or mission into reality and persuading people at all levels of the organization to pull together to achieve common goals."[14] We at Reed Library have been experimenting with team management for the past four years in an effort to improve communication, adapt to increasing use of computers, and improve service to our patrons. The following is a summary of my reaction to this style of management from the point of view of team member and former Team Leader.

The idea of a team organization was presented to the staff by Susan Besemer when she became our Director after she consulted with librarians and other staff members. This frankly appealed to me because I have participated in teams all my life and know from experience that more can be accomplished with a team effort than can be accomplished alone. As a kid in grade school, I had a "gang" of boys and girls of various ages who played sandlot baseball, kick-the-can–all the street games in a small town in upstate New York. I sang in church choirs and school choruses and I played intramural softball, volleyball and basketball in Junior High. I acted in Children's Theater and in school plays. As a college student, I team-studied with other students, discussing ideas and receiving feedback and support. As an adult, wife, mother, teacher, church and community worker, I enjoyed the results of group work and suffered from "trying to go it alone" at times.

The method Sue encouraged us to use was to define our own roles within the framework of the team structure. Our team consists of the acquisitions/serials librarian, bibliographic control librarian, systems librarian, special collections professional and the head clerk in Bibliographic Control. Though we are not strictly Technical Services, that is our title: the Technical Services Team. We spent the first few months determining how to function as a team, what relationship the team has to the Team Leader and to the Director, what relationship our team has to the Public Access Team. We discussed meeting times and places, what to bring to the team and what to solve in our own areas. Our first Team Leader had the difficult role of presiding over all of this agonizing. He was very busy facilitating discussion, and clarifying us to the Director and the Director to us. It was a dynamic, if frustrating, first two years.

I was chosen as the second Team Leader and brought my own ideas to the role, encouraged by the Director to do so. I read the literature and attended management workshops, sharing the information learned with my colleagues. Some of the librarians met with me periodically on a volunteer basis so we could get to know each other individually. We were given the task of establishing a five-year plan as part of a campus-wide assessment-based-planning activity. Using the brainstorming technique, we created plans for each of our areas and, in cooperation with the Public Access Team and the Director, for the whole Library. We also implemented the use of consensus in our decision-making.

One of the hardest tasks each of us seemed to have was in sharing problems and problem-solving. Our hierarchical background made it difficult for us to give up autonomy in our own departments. We worked hard to overcome this and to be honest with each other–supportive, but honest. This is not to say that we didn't have some vigorous disagreements, but we worked them out together.

One current example of team problem-solving is the issue of staffing our Special Collections Room in the Library during the times when the archivist is not on duty. Both teams have met to determine procedures, hours, and people to provide service. An example of successful teamwork across team lines is the group that does the planning to implement our automated library system. This group, which I chair, is primarily for problem-solving and meets weekly to work out procedures and problems arising from our online system, PALS. My own department, Bibliographic Control, meets weekly to iron out difficulties and set goals and priorities. We often meet with other area groups to solve inter-area problems, such as Circulation and Acquisitions/Serials. At these meetings, the Chair is the facilitator and everyone has a chance to express opinions and ideas. Each is respected for his or her contribution and expertise. This is a far cry from the old hierarchy.

However, we are not without problems. Many of us still haven't accepted the team approach and some still say "nothing has changed." I have noted that these are the ones who do not participate without being forcefully encouraged. They are still using the old "send a memo" approach or "just tell me what it is you want me to do and I'll do it" line. We also have some who "hate meetings" and resist attending and when they do attend do not participate. These folks have plenty to say "off the cuff," but not where it can be examined. This is not to say that these people don't do their jobs or contribute in many ways. They just haven't learned that a team works only if you work it.

The future looks promising, however, and those of us who believe in the teams are working hard to bring the others in. We are working hard, also, to respect each other for what we can contribute. As far as the actual organization of the Library after the five-year experiment is concluded, I don't know. Many ideas have been kicked around: making one big team (because we have a very small staff and maybe we shouldn't be separated), hiring an assistant director and keeping the small groups and eliminating the large teams, or reorganizing the teams to include different members. There are many possible solutions. Choosing one is our next step in this continuing process of learning to manage ourselves and our Library.

BARBARA KITTLE: A TEAM MEMBER'S VIEW

As a member of the Public Access Team from its inception, I have been able to watch and participate in the development of this managerial concept. I have had no interest in becoming a Team Leader and am content to be "just" a team member. Being "just" a team member is not an easy task as team members play a crucial part in the success or failure of the team.

Over the last four years I have served under three Team Leaders. As in any group of people the personalities of its members play an important role in how the group works. The same is true for teams, and especially the personalities of the Team Leaders. There are, as you would expect, many differences among them. Therefore, my first job as a team member is to adjust to each Team Leader as they begin their term.

The three Team Leaders I have worked with have approached their jobs with different expectations of what they were supposed to do and what was expected of the team members. For example, let's look at minute taking at the meetings of the Public Access Team. We started out with the first Team Leader rotating the task of taking and distributing the minutes of our weekly team meeting with all team members taking turns. The next Team Leader decided that he would take the minutes himself and then the team decided that it didn't want to take minutes at all. The third Team Leader was appointed and started her term with a new strategy: agendas instead of minutes. Right now we are not taking minutes or doing an agenda. The other team, the Technical Services Team, has always taken minutes of their meetings and would very much like the Public Access Team to do minutes as well. It is hard to predict what the next Team Leader will do.

Another very important aspect of working with a team is the need for communication. As a member of a team I depend on the Team Leader to convey news and information to me. The Team Leader has direct contact with the Director and the other Team Leaders and needs to pass on pertinent information to the team. Minutes of the Team Leader Meetings are the most effective method of passing this information on to others. If, when we read the minutes, we find something interesting or noteworthy, we can bring it up for discussion at the team meeting. We depend on the Team Leader to tell us what's going on. When this doesn't happen, there is the feeling of being left out in the cold.

It is also a good idea to make sure that the team understands its role in the structure of the Library. The team structure had been in operation years before it became clear to me that the teams make recommendations; they do not make policy decisions. An example of this was the Public Access Team's recommendation that the

Library be open regular library hours on Easter Sunday. When the hours were announced for that semester the hours for Easter were not the regular Sunday hours. Somewhere the hours were changed and the team knew nothing about the change until it was published in the campus hours bulletin. The need to make sure that the role of the team is well defined and that the lines of communication between the Team Leader and the team are open and ongoing should be made clear very early in the formation of the teams.

Participation in groups other than the team is another very important aspect of the Library's organization. There's a staff meeting covering almost every area of library operations; reference, collection development, library faculty, and circulation, to name just a few, all have regularly scheduled meetings through the week or month. These groups also make recommendations to the Director as well as decisions on non-policy matters. My supervisor signs my time sheets, not the Team Leader. It's the Collection Development Committee that decides the fate of new serial subscriptions and the library faculty has input on personnel decisions. But the team is where discussion and recommendations come for requests for travel moneys in support of attendance at conferences and workshops. It is the Director who has final say on how much travel money is given each request. The Director and each librarian meet once a month to discuss anything on their minds. If I didn't have this monthly meeting with the Director there would be very little direct contact between myself and the Director.

As a member of a team it is important that you actively participate in the team to ensure that decisions and recommendations coming from the team are made with input from all involved. Realize that you do have a say in what goes on in your library even if you do not make the decisions. The most useful means of communication has been the minutes of the Team Leaders Meetings, especially when a Team Leader does not bring something up for discussion himself or herself. Without the objectives and responsibilities of the team clearly defined your team will not function as the group was intended to function. And lastly, I see the Team Leader as the key to the team. The Team Leader will not be permanent so you will have to adjust to a new Team Leader regularly. The personality and leadership style of each Team Leader has a definite effect on the team. Without quality leadership and a Team Leader who is working for and with the team this concept will not work as it was envisioned to work.

SARAH DORSEY: A NEWCOMER'S VIEW

I am a believer in communication in any and all relationships, be they personal or work related. The number of interpretations of any given situation is at least as great as the number of people involved. It can only help in the long run if people feel free to make comments and observations and know how their statements are being received by others. Smooth operations in an environment as multilayered as a library can only occur when these layers are in constant contact with one another. The right hand needs to know what the left hand is doing.

In work situations there is a built-in inequality between supervisors and their workers which must be carefully offset with constant vigilance. This inequality or "power differential" can cause a breakdown in communication. Then small misunderstandings can grow into large problems and bring operations to a standstill or simply make the work environment unpleasant and tense.

One of the major benefits of any experiment in management should be either a maintenance of good communication lines or their improvement. It is my observation in my year at Reed Library in Fredonia that communication has increased and I theorize that this is, in part, due to the management experiment now in progress called team management.

You have just read various points of view and observations relating to our experiment. Sue Besemer, Carrie Niles and Barbara Kittle have been involved with team management from its inception. My reason for being included is to provide a fresh point of view. My position at Reed Library is unique in that, as Music Librarian, I have reasons to deal with both Public Services and Technical Services and attended both team meetings for a short time. I soon realized that I did not have time for any extra meetings, but it did allow me to see both teams in operation and compare them.

I arrived in the middle of a move from the old building into the temporary headquarters in our new addition. Anyone who remembers his or her first month on a job will remember the thrill of every day feeling like five days, and every moment a new surprise being revealed to you. So, I was ready to mix into my personal chaos the added anarchy of a move. My new colleagues, however, although having planned as well as possible were surprised by the amount of emotional and physical energy necessary to uproot themselves from an area some had known for twenty years. Suffice it to say that there was an unusual amount of stress on all employees especially when you add the anxiety of dealing with disgruntled patrons whose study areas have been disrupted.

After asking what the teams were all about, I was given a document which outlined the set-up of the new structure and encouraged questions. After reading the document, I asked various colleagues what they thought the teams were all about and got a variety of answers. Some of the discrepancies between answers depended on which team they were on, but most showed a general fuzziness of definition.

One of the problems with the teams as they are now is that they perpetuate an old worn out line of division in libraries between technical and public services. Ideally, that wall will ultimately be broken down and free exchange will occur. With this flaw in mind, I will now compare the two teams.

As far as meeting protocol goes, in the team to which I belong, the Public Access Team, there was no agenda and no minutes were taken. In the Technical Services Team there was no agenda, but minutes were taken. Each member of the Technical Services team was asked if they had anything to discuss before the meeting, a sort of on-the-spot agenda. The agenda for the Public Access Team seemed to be going over the most recent Team Leader Meeting minutes and whatever got mentioned before the meeting ended.

I sensed frustration and lack of openness on the Public Access Team whereas the Technical Services Team felt more like an open forum. There were loud and often spirited exchanges in the Technical Services Team, but I felt people were generally satisfied with the discussions and felt their views were heard. The Public Access Team, however, was loud with unspoken issues which clouded conversation when it did happen. It seemed that communication was not as free on this side of the Library. It became clear that there was history here of which I was not aware that was affecting the team members' behavior.

When the period for reevaluation of the teams started in January of 1992, a new topic of conversation was humming at Reed Library: the team structure itself; the team make-up; how, after four years, it was working; and how to improve it. Because the teams themselves would be affected, it was thought that the Library Faculty Governance would be a good preliminary forum for discussing the team structure as it is "outside" the structure.

Items discussed at this Faculty Governance meeting included: a team for the support staff, or more representation for them; the use of audio cassette tapes on team building;[15] change in the Team Leader duties; and rearrangement of the team personnel.

Although their styles were different, the two teams reached similar conclusions in their appraisal of the situation. Both teams realized that they were confused about the purpose and definition of the teams. The Technical Services Team worked on examining what the team was. They listened to some of the team building tapes together and discussed them. They brought up issues such as the fact that they felt that a lack of introduction, education and training at the beginning of the team implementation had impeded its progress. They realized that communication was not always clear and confusion arose on what was an appropriate topic for team discussion. Was the team advisory or did it have power to change policy? Again the concern for the support staff representation and input was expressed. There were discussions regarding the meaning of consensus and the possibility of more team lunches to enhance the group's working relationship.

The Public Access Team discussion was more animated and focussed. The issue which emerged was a general frustration with the function of the teams and how they relate to the Director and why they exist. I felt that a flood gate was released at this meeting, that long-held resentments were finally voiced. What emerged was a basic question: What has the team decided in the last four years? As I was not around for this time period, I listened to my colleagues come to the conclusion that very few concrete items had been decided at the team level and a clear definition of the function of the teams was necessary. The Public Access Team recommended that a joint team meeting be held so that both teams could discuss the situation together.

The first of these joint team meetings happened in January. At this meeting both teams agreed that the Director should be invited to the next joint meeting so that she could clarify her view of the teams' functions with both teams present. A number of issues were clarified at this meeting which occurred at the beginning of February. The relationship of the area meetings and team meetings was discussed. Much of what employees thought should be "decided" at the team level were actually area decisions or implementations such as Bibliographic Instruction by the Reference Staff or the implementation of the automated library system which touched everyone on the staff in different ways.

It became clear that the Director's definition of the teams was more of an administrative function than an active function. The actions (or specific "decisions") should come from the areas, not the teams, the Director clarified. The function of the teams is advisory, recommending to the leaders who then recommend to the Director who then (if necessary) recommends to the Vice President. This appeared to be a different definition of the team function from the previous understanding of some of the staff. I did enjoy the opportunity for a shared meeting which broke down the old Technical Services/Public Services wall. We continue to have joint team meetings monthly.

There are still many aspects which need to be clarified in the ongoing experiment, but one concrete advance already accomplished through examination of the teams was the reestablishment of area meetings. Communication within each library department has increased. Circulation, Reference, Bibliographic Control, and Acquisitions all meet on a regular basis again and this certainly enhances the functioning of the Library. There had been some confusion as to the need for area meetings if the teams existed. This is now clearer.

We are facing yet another challenging time with the renovation on the old building, which is scheduled to be completed by the fall of 1993. With the experience of the first move behind us, we hope to face this time with increased respect for the amount of stress we will all sustain, and be gentle with ourselves and one another. Part of this gentleness is taking the time to hear what others are saying and responding carefully.

The team concept has influenced a variety of staff activities. As far as the reevaluation of the teams goes, preparation for a presentation on team management sparked yet another flurry of discussion about the teams. On a scholarly note, an article published by Barbara Kittle raised our consciousness in this area.[16] In a lighter vein, a "recovering" Team Leader has created a "management tool" based on a recent popular movie. It is called the "Wayne's World Management Matrix" and it traces the origin and path of suggestions through three categories: "Excellent, Party On!" "No Way; Way!" and "Hurl!"

We are three fourths of the way through this year of reassessment, and the outcome has yet to be seen. However the teams evolve or whether they even dissolve, the process of examining this management structure has increased communication at Reed Library. There is no other job at which I can remember such openness of discussion on the topic of who our next "boss," or Team Leader, might be, or how we think the organizational structure of the Library might benefit from a rearrangement of personnel. Given that any healthy organization is organic and changing, just as people are, the need to keep in touch will never cease. Perhaps team management can help us communicate more efficiently.

TEAMWORK SUCCESS STORIES: THE DIRECTOR'S PERSPECTIVE

As has been mentioned by others, the team concept has extended far beyond its use in formal management teams. I am especially excited, as Director, by successful projects that operate across team lines. To return to a question posed earlier, and perhaps to the bottom line reason for implementing a team management structure in an academic library, does this system work more effectively for us?

Three short vignettes can serve as modest examples of how the team concept has allowed for more thorough and efficient analysis of problems, and for resolving problems using the input of all of the people involved. In a traditional organizational structure, a manager could have had much less confidence that all people concerned were truly involved in the resolution of the issue. The first example is a problem located only in one team, Technical Services, while the other two instances are examples of library-wide teamwork.

The first example shows how the Technical Services Team solved a small problem on its own. The effective resolution of this problem, however, has important implications regarding the standing of the Library in the College community.

It was noticed that book request cards, completed by faculty members to request purchases, were being returned to the requester much later than the books themselves were on the shelves. Faculty were led to believe that it was taking much longer to acquire, catalog, and process their requests than was in fact the case. The Technical Services Team worked for several sessions, involving librarians and clerks in both Acquisitions and Bibliographic Control to locate bottlenecks slowing return of the cards. Both units reviewed long-standing processes, and without outside intervention found several steps that could be modified to expedite the handling of the cards, to match the speed of the books themselves through the Technical Services processes.

Another example also caused concern because of its possible negative reflection on the apparent effectiveness of the Library. This was brought to our attention by a faculty member in our School of Music. She pointed out that our processing of record discs and CDs was obscuring some of the information included on the record jacket and the label. While this seems like a Technical Services problem, actually it was a situation that also involved the Circulation area, since the placement of barcode and other labels on the materials is of concern to them. A small group from each team, again involving both librarians and support staff sat together and worked out the details of how to improve our processing of music recordings. In fact, in this instance, we went on to notice a need to amplify contents notes for music materials on our local computer access system. We even found a retired librarian living in the community to take on the project as a volunteer! Without the teams' taking ownership of the problem and making a commitment to work it out, the incident could have caused annoyance and resentment in the minds of faculty and students who need to locate and use sometimes obscure works, identified only on the record jackets or labels of the discs.

The third incident is a happy story about an opportunity that achieved a very positive service reputation for the Library from a grant project on campus. Interdisciplinary researchers from the natural and social sciences came to us with a request for extra service. They needed additional help to achieve the goals that they had established when their grant funding was awarded. They were willing to compensate the Library for the enhanced level of service that they were requesting, if we could meet their requirements in a timely way. They needed intensive bibliographic searching of our own materials and those of research libraries, finding appropriate materials to support this interdisciplinary project, and obtaining articles and other resources through Interlibrary Loan or document delivery services. These extra services had to be prompt, for the time line of the grant was short. The project involved our Reference librarians, Interlibrary Loan, Circulation, and even Acquisitions, since the researchers wanted us to find and acquire some sample issues of periodicals for them to evaluate. We needed to present a high and consistent level of service for them. Several meetings with library faculty and staff who would be likely to be asked by the researchers for assistance got everybody on board. One never knew where or when the researchers might appear: at the Information Desk, in Interlibrary Loan, or at the copy machines. They became familiar faces over the three-month project period. At the conclusion of the Library's portion of the project, the researchers were absolutely gushy in their praise of our services. Only through the coordinated effort possible in a team environment could we have met their expectations. We all profit from such team efforts, and we all share in the glory when our hard work is appreciated.

A key issue of the success of any team structure lies in the increased levels of personal responsibility that are both required and provided under a team approach. Particular jobs are no longer the isolated territory of just one person, even in a small library like ours. Librarians and support staff are growing in their appreciation of their own responsibility and in their respect for the work that their colleagues are performing.

With that increasing willingness to assume responsibility comes an increased trust from others. Trust from colleagues grows as each project is successfully completed, on time. The Director trusts the library faculty and staff to get the job done, and they likewise trust her leadership ability and her judgment. As we've worked together over the past four years, that mutual trust has grown.

The small examples related above give some specific details of how teamwork has helped Reed Library. More profoundly important are two massive projects which would have been impossible without the flexibility, improved communications, and increased level of responsibility generated by teamwork. In the past four years, with a staff numbering fewer than thirty people, we have taken on two important projects to move the Library forward in the provision of information services. We have implemented a long-needed library automation project which is nearly completed. We have also planned and implemented a $7.3 million building and renovation program also to be completed in 1993. These were challenging projects; ones that elicited professional growth in all staff members, and an increasing reliance upon one another.

When we complete our experiment in organizational structure next year, we may decide to continue as we have so far, to adjust our structure, or to change it altogether. The team structure has served us well during this interval. It has been an agent of change, allowing us to begin the process of transformation from a traditional, highly authoritarian work environment to one where library faculty and staff have the knowledge and self-confidence to know what needs to be done, and the sense of professionalism and responsibility that urges them to go ahead and do their best.

NOTES

1. W. Edwards Deming, *Out of the Crisis* (Cambridge, Mass.: Massachusetts Institute of Technology, Center for Advanced Engineering Study, 1986).

2. Two examples of important books from this decade are: Douglas McGregor, *The Human Side of Enterprise* (New York: McGraw-Hill, 1960), and Rensis Likert, *New Patterns of Management* (New York: McGraw-Hill, 1961).

3. Two examples from the 1970s and 1980s include: Chris Argyris and Donald A. Schon, *Organizational Learning: A Theory of Action Perspective* (Reading, MA: Addison-Wesley, 1978), and Charles A. Aubrey and Patricia K. Felkins, *Teamwork: Involving People in Quality and Productivity Improvement* (Milwaukee, WI: Quality Press, American Society for Quality Control, 1988).

4. Joan Bechtel, "Collegial Management Breeds Success," *American Libraries* 12 (November 1981): 605-607.

5. Dorothy H. Cieslicki, "A New Status Model for Academic Librarians," *The Journal of Academic Librarianship* 8:2 (May 1982): 76-81.

6. Joan M. Bechtel, "Rotation Day Reflections: How Collegial Management Works at Dickinson College," *College & Research Libraries News*, 10 (November 1985): 551-555.

7. Charles Martell and Joan D. Kunselman, "QWL Strategies: Involvement = Commitment," *Journal of Academic Librarianship*, 10:3 (July 1984): 158-160.

8. Hannelore Rader, "Creative Library Leadership for the 1990s: Using Team Management to Ensure Two-Way Communication in an Academic Library," ERIC document ED304137, Paper presented at the Library Administration and Management Association President's Program at the Annual Convention of the American Library Association, New Orleans, LA, July 10, 1988.

9. Gisela Webb, "Preparing Staff for Participative Management," *Wilson Library Bulletin* 62 (May 1988): 50-52.

10. Jennifer Cargill, "Integrating Public and Technical Services Staffs to Implement the New Mission of Libraries," *Journal of Library Administration* 104 (1989): 21-31.

11. Katherine W. Hawkins, "Team Development and Management," *Library Administration & Management* 4 (Winter 1990): 11-15.

12. Maureen Sullivan, "A New Leadership Paradigm: Empowering Library Staff and Improving Performance," *Journal of Library Administration* 14:2 (1991): 73-85.

13. See note 8 above.

14. Richard S. Wellins, William C. Byham and Jean Wilson, *Empowered Teams: Creating Self-Directed Work Groups That Improve Quality, Productivity and Participation* (San Francisco: Jossey-Bass Publishers, 1991), 86.

15. Mark Sanborn, *Teambuilding* (audio cassettes) (Boulder, Colorado: Career Track Publications, 1989).

16. Alan Zaremba and Barbara Kittle, "The Value of Organizational Teams: A Study in Team Intervention," *The Quality Observer: The International New Magazine of Quality* (February 1992): 1, 14-15.

APPENDIX A

REED LIBRARY'S
TEAM STRUCTURE
AT A GLANCE

Two Teams:

* Technical Services (5 librarians, 1 clerk)

    Acquisitions
    Bibliographic Control
    Systems
    Interlibrary Loan
    Archives/Special Collections
    Senior Library Clerk

* Public Access (6 librarians, 1 clerk)

    Circulation
    Reference
    Music
    Collection Development
    Senior Library Clerk

Team Leader:

* Each Team headed by a Team Leader
* Two year term
* Appointed by Director
* Receives stipend
* Term is staggered with the other Team Leader

Meetings:

* Each area (Circulation, Acquisitions, etc.) meets weekly for planning and information sharing
* Team meets weekly, recommends to Director and/or other Team
* Team Leaders Meeting weekly with Director (open to visitors)
* Joint Team Meeting (both Teams) once a month

Director meets:
- * Every couple of months with full staff
- * Standing appointment monthly with each librarian
- * Standing appointment weekly with each Team Leader
- * Standing weekly Team Leaders Meeting

What do the Teams do?
- * Plan and implement goals
- * Share information among areas
- * Make decisions on issues which involve the Team's areas
- * Make recommendations on policy issues which involve the whole Library

Total Quality Management: A Mindset and Method to Stimulate Change

Janet A. Mullen

INTRODUCTION

If you have not heard of Total Quality Management (TQM), you simply have not been paying attention. TQM has received wide notice in the United States in the last decade and public and private organizations alike are adopting this new approach to managing the process of improving themselves. Even universities, typically known to be skeptical about applying business concepts to higher education, have adopted the TQM model. The American Association for Higher Education (AAHE) began "paying attention" to TQM in 1989 (Marchese, 1992). Other academic professional associations have realized the importance and relevance of TQM to higher education. If you attended a professional meeting in the last year, chances are, TQM had a prominent place on the agenda, drew standing room only crowds, and may have been the focus of the keynote address of the guest speaker. Moreover, some academic professional associations have sponsored TQM-specific seminars for their members such as the National Association of College and

---

Janet A. Mullen is Associate Director, Student Health, Arizona State University, Tempe, AZ.

[Haworth co-indexing entry note]: "Total Quality Management: A Mindset and Method to Stimulate Change." Mullen, Janet A. Co-published simultaneously in the *Journal of Library Administration* (The Haworth Press, Inc.) Vol. 18, No. 3/4, 1993, pp. 91-108; and: *Catalysts for Change: Managing Libraries in the 1990s* (ed: Gisela M. von Dran and Jennifer Cargill) The Haworth Press, Inc., 1993, pp. 91-108. Multiple copies of this article/chapter may be purchased from The Haworth Document Delivery Center [1-800-3-HAWORTH; 9:00 a.m. - 5:00 p.m. (EST)].

© 1993 by The Haworth Press, Inc. All rights reserved.

University Business Officers (NACUBO) did in December 1991 and March 1992.

What is all the enthusiasm about and why should those of us in higher education consider adopting a Total Quality Management philosophy? The purpose of this article is to review the total quality management movement and process, and examine the application of TQM to enterprises within higher education.

HIGHER EDUCATION IS IN A PREDICAMENT

Much of what has been written recently about higher education is somewhat dismal. We have become all too familiar with the challenges of declining resources. Layoffs, elimination of academic programs, declining faculty and staff morale, increased tuition and other user fees have had a negative impact on maintaining high quality institutions. Meanwhile, new expectations have been imposed upon us by legislators, alumni and the general public. Higher education has been called upon to be more accountable in its use of state appropriated dollars, to defend faculty workloads, to improve undergraduate teaching, and to increase admissions' standards while maintaining or improving access to institutions. Furthermore, as improvements in technology abound, and services outside our institutions become more customer-oriented and responsive, the service or auxiliary sectors of campus receive increasing pressure to provide immediate and comprehensive service to students, and to faculty and staff as well.

Ironically, in a time when budgets are decreasing, higher education's customer expectations are rising. Daniel Seymour (1992), in his book *On Q: Causing Quality in Higher Education*, discusses his belief that significant change does not occur in organizations unless pressure from outside the organization, prompts it to do so. He cites four motivating forces for change in higher education today: (1) survival in an increasingly competitive environment; (2) the escalation of costs of doing business; (3) a trend to make organizations more accountable for their actions and outcomes; and (4) a blurring of the distinction between products and services (p. 3).

First, many institutions of higher education understand that they are in a highly competitive environment. It is more difficult to attract and to retain faculty and students. Comparisons of colleges are provided annually by many well-known weekly magazines. And institutions compete for public funds with health care agencies, public transportation, prisons and elementary and secondary schools.

Secondly, the costs of doing business are escalating. Tuition increases for many schools, have outpaced the inflation rate in recent years. To compound the problem, many campuses experienced rapid growth in the two decades preceding the 1990s. The costs of maintaining this infrastructure is burdensome. Add to this the rapid growth in technology and the building of an information infrastructure, and it is not surprising that higher education is feeling a financial squeeze.

Most institutions have experienced the third motivating force for change. As resources diminish, parents, legislators and governing boards want evidence that dollars are being used appropriately and effectively. The call for assessment of undergraduate education, and ability to show positive outcomes is evidence of the drive for accountability.

The final factor to provide impetus for change is the blurring of the distinction between products and services. Seymour shows that consumers do not look at products and services differently, they tend to see all companies and organizations in the business of providing service. They also tend to define quality and a good "product" differently than the institution may, or the faculty might. Providing quality is exceeding the technical requirements of the customer. Consequently, higher education must engage in service improvement. Even though the student-to-faculty ratio may be strong, the faculty have impressive credentials, and the library has an immense collection, the institution may not be meeting the needs of the students. The foundation and the technical requirements for a quality education have been provided, but the deficiency is in the delivery of these goods.

Seymour (1992) acknowledges that having the motivation to change is not enough. An organization or individual must have a means to make the change happen. If a means is not present, the organization will experience decline and fear, with no visible escape from the milieu.

TQM MAY BE THE ANSWER

The message is clear: "do more with less." So why look at TQM now, when so much is being scrutinized and so much more is at stake. This is precisely why universities should consider it. In an August 1992 article in the Chronicle of Higher Education, Theodore J. Marchese suggests that TQM is a viable approach for colleges and universities to consider:

> People are realizing that when we get to the other side of the recession, it isn't going to be business as usual. We have a significant problem with the public confidence and the way we use resources. People are looking for answers, and Total Quality presents itself as a possible solution. (Mangan 1992, p. A25)

The promises of TQM are that an organization can do more, but in a different way, that quality does not increase costs, it actually costs less, and that involving everyone in TQM can have positive impact on employee morale and job satisfaction. TQM certainly seems to offer an antidote for what currently is ailing higher education by providing a way to improve the ability to satisfy the customer, at a lower cost than present methods.

Unfortunately or fortunately, depending on your vantage point, the change requires an institutional transformation in the way we get things done, and what we believe about getting things done. It requires not only doing it differently, but believing that there is a better way of doing business and practicing it throughout the organization, by every employee at every level. TQM is said to be as much mindset as method, and many believe that it is a new management philosophy, bolstered by new tools and a method of solving problems that will transform the enterprise in which we are engaged.

THE INSTITUTIONS THAT LEAD THE WAY

Total Quality Management emerged from organizations primarily involved in manufacturing a tangible product. More recently, it has received attention from businesses involved in producing services, and in the last decade it has been applied to higher education. Fox

Valley Technical College (FVTC) was one of the first post secondary institutions to adopt TQM (Bemowski, 1991). At the request of a local businessman, FVTC developed and offered a course on TQM in 1985. Soon thereafter, they began incorporating the TQM approach in aspects of administering the operational goals of the institution. FVTC's teams have made several improvements to processes within the college including course scheduling, and also developed a comprehensive in-service program for new adjunct faculty. FVTC also has established the Academy for Quality in Education. Expertise and insight is shared through workshops and seminars which focus on applying TQM concepts and tools in an academic organization.

Oregon State University (OSU) has also become well-known as a pioneer in implementing TQM in a university setting (Coate, 1990). What began in 1990 with ten departments, has been expanded to a goal of supporting 400 teams throughout the university by 1995. The pilot team results are impressive. The Physical Plant Team reduced the average duration of remodeling jobs by 23 percent, the Business Affairs Team reduced the number of journal vouchers returned to departments for error correction by 94 percent, and another Business Affairs Team decreased the number of days to process grant/contract documents by 10 percent. This ambitious university is striving to be recognized nationally for its efforts and has as a goal, achieving the Malcolm Baldridge award by 1994. This award was established by the U.S. Congress in 1987 to recognize organizations that have successfully implemented TQM. Motorola, Cadillac, Federal Express and Xerox have been successful in attaining the award.

In addition to individual campuses, North Dakota is known to be the first state university system to adopt the TQM model (Bemowski, 1991). This is quite an undertaking since the system includes eleven individual campuses as well as the Chancellor's Office. In North Dakota, they refer to their program as TQI for Total Quality Improvement, (rather than management) recognizing that all members of the organization, not just the managers, must embrace total quality or the program will not succeed. In presentations given by Ellen Earle Chaffee (1991), the vice chancellor for academic affairs, to introduce colleges and universities to TQM, she cites three major values of TQM that are germane to higher education. These are values that echo many college and university mission statements: people, knowledge and continuous improvement.

People are certainly higher education's greatest resource. Without faculty and the infrastructure of people who support them, we would not be able to convey our products: education and research. We also value the people who are our customers. However, the problem is, we do not listen to them, but instead provide what we think they need. Second, we value knowledge. It is, after all, our goal to seek new knowledge through research and to communicate our findings. Finally, what are education and research if not continuous improvement? It follows then, that the TQM should not be a difficult philosophy for many in higher education to buy into, yet the way in which it is applied to our organizations is unsettling to some. Robert Carothers, the president of the University of Rhode Island, astutely addressed this concern in a 1992 article for the AAHE Bulletin, and gave an eloquent defense for supporting the implementation of TQM in higher education:

> I have come to believe that introducing lessons learned in the TQM movement to the academy is not to bring an alien presence into our culture. Rather, it is to give form and clarity to values that are already very much a part of our community. (p. 7)

THE TOTAL QUALITY GURUS

A discussion of TQM would be incomplete without some mention of those who inspired the effort. Several men are credited with the total quality movement in the United States, including Philip Crosby, Dr. W. Edwards Deming, and Dr. Joseph Juran. In addition, Kaoro Ishikawa of Japan is often mentioned as having greatly influenced the thinking of both Juran and Deming.

Although U.S. citizens are most often associated with developing the concept of TQM, the application of the method is associated with Japan. W. Edwards Deming is the statistician who has promoted the model here and abroad, but actually began working with the Japanese, almost immediately after WWII. In 1947 he was asked to Japan by the staff of General Douglas MacArthur to conduct a census of the war torn country. In 1950, Deming gave an eight-day seminar on statistical quality control for managers and engineers. He returned there nearly every year for 40 years (Gabor 1990). Not until 1978, when U.S. automotive executives traveled to Japan to look at the advances made in the industry, did many in this country become acquainted with Deming and his reputation. In 1981, Donald Peterson who was then the president at Ford Motor Company, asked Deming to assist his organization (Walton 1986). Deming's Fourteen Points for implementing TQM are widely used and referred to by proponents of TQM. For reference, they appear in total at the end of this article (Deming, 1986).

Peter Drucker credits Deming with supplying the scientific methodology for analyzing the process (Gabor, 1990). Deming views employees as a resource, not a cost, and believes in a democratic partnership in the workplace. He often states in his seminars that the goal is to "get the customer to come back and bring a friend." Deming also believes it is more useful to ask questions than to give answers, something any employee would appreciate from upper level management. This is in part what won him the respect of the Japanese. Instead of making assumptions about what would or would not work in their post-war ravaged country, he actually listened to them with great respect for their knowledge about their own culture and condition. In his dealings with the Japanese, he modeled the approach he expects managers to use with employees. Managers should meet with and listen to the employees on the front line and demonstrate respect for what they know about the operation and the processes. Then ask the customer what they want and need, and not only meet those needs but exceed them.

In 1954, Dr. Joseph M. Juran visited Japan and lectured on the roles of top and mid-level managers in promoting Quality Control. He initiated the important transition from analyzing the technology to critically examining the commitment from the highest level of management. This initiated a significant shift from inspection of the product to examining the overall process. He believed that the technical aspects of quality improvement had been mastered, but not the management aspects of quality improvement. Top level management had to be included to deal with problems that were interdepartmental. Just as managers need training in controlling financial activities of the firm, they also need instruction in managing quality. Juran was the first to evaluate quality from a big picture point of view. In addition, he believes that there is a point of diminishing returns, rather than purporting that all efforts to improve quality are free.

Philip Crosby became well known in academic circles in the 1960s for promoting a "zero-defects" approach to production. This was during a time when he was in charge of quality for the Pershing Missile project at Martin Corporation. He left that position to work for ITT as a corporate vice president and director of quality. In 1979 he formed Philip Crosby and Associates. In the United States, Crosby's reputation preceded the other quality gurus because of his best-selling book, *Quality is Free* (1979).

Ishikawa believes that success depends on participation by all and describes TQM as a thought revolution in management that begins and ends with education (Ishikawa, 1985). He also posits that the success of Quality Control in Japan is somewhat related to the culture dominated by one race, and one language, making the thought revolution easier to implement. He believes it takes 10 years to see effects of TQM and unfortunately, Western culture is not patient enough to wait for the results. According to Ishikawa (1985), quality control is:

> to develop, design, produce and service a quality product which is most economical, most useful, and always satisfactory to the customer. (p. 44)

Deming, Juran and Crosby each has a unique list of guidelines that expound the TQM mindset and methods. Although there are differences among them, each approach shares the concept of continuous process improvement. In an effort to assimilate the ideas of the most widely-quoted TQM gurus, Lawrence Sherr (1991), a professor of business at the University of Kansas, discerned five common themes of TQM:

1. Customer Focus
2. Systematic Improvement of Operations
3. Develop Human Resources

4. Long-term Thinking
5. Commitment to Quality

These appear to be fairly straightforward and reasonable suggestions. Then why has there been a delay for a significant number of colleges and universities to adopt TQM?

APPLYING TQM TO HIGHER EDUCATION

The TQM proponents on the campuses that have implemented the approach, report that these five caveats can be implemented appropriately within higher education. However, they do acknowledge TQM is much easier to implement in the areas where customers and their needs are more easily defined, that is, the service sectors of a campus. Some institutions are wringing their hands about how to apply this in the academic side of the house. This did not suppress one enterprising associate professor of forestry engineering at Oregon State University who decided TQM was worthwhile, and applicable to the classroom. He asked his students to participate in a TQM team to help him improve his teaching. Based on analysis of the data gathered through student surveys, he received many useful suggestions from the TQM team comprised of his customers (Mangan, 1992).

Customer Emphasis

In TQM, the focus on the customer is of paramount importance. A first step for TQM teams is to define all of the internal and external customers for a given process. In addition to the traditional concept of customer as someone who is external to the organization and receives a good or service, TQM broadens the concept of customer to include each employee in the organization who is the recipient of work completed by another employee.

In an organization where TQM has taken hold, each individual adds value to the product prior to sending it to the next individual in the process chain. The belief is that if you are not dealing directly with the customer, you are providing something for someone who is. For example, an administrator supplies a secretary with instructions for completing a task. If the instructions are not clear or are incomplete, it is likely that the task will have to be "redone." In this scenario, the secretary is a customer of the administrator who has not provided a quality product, that is, good instructions to complete the product or task.

In turn, the administrator is a customer of the secretary. The secretary produces a service for the administrator by managing the ratio of appointments to desk time daily. If the calendaring was performed ineptly, the service provided would be poor and the consequences negative. Imagine the improvement in work processes and employee morale if more people viewed their bosses, subordinates and co-workers as customers.

Linda Thor (1992), president of Rio Salado Community College in Phoenix, Arizona, describes the payoff for attending to the internal customers in the following way:

> "TQM . . . forges a chain of flawless processes leading directly to the satisfied customers" and "TQM ultimately means shared responsibility and shared rewards for everyone." (p. 13)

The importance of satisfying external customers was addressed by Dalton Kehoe, in a presentation to the National Association of College and University Business Officers Conference in Toronto in July, 1992. He referred to a study conducted by the Technical Assistance Research Projects group from Washington, D.C., which reveals some important characteristics of customers, especially those who are not happy with a product or service. The data show that for customers, the power of frustration is far greater than the power of satisfaction. Another significant finding was that an organization may never get a second chance to provide a favorable impression because:

- 96% of unhappy customers never complain, but . . .
- 90% never return, and . . .
- Each one tells at least 7 others
- 13% tell at least 20 others
- It costs five times as much time, energy and money to attract a new customer as it does to retain an existing one
- Each happy customer tells at least five others (p. 4)

Quality should be defined by the needs of the customer. Unfortunately in higher education, assumptions are made about customer needs that may not be on target. To discover the needs of the customer, TQM teams survey them and ask them to identify their quality requirements and preferences. Deming encourages organizations to go beyond asking the customer for feedback, although he acknowledges this as a necessary step (Gabor, 1990). He believes you need to stay one step ahead of your customers, anticipating rather than reacting to their needs:

> No advance is made by the customer. None asked for electricity, or the automobile, the camera, pneumatic tires, or the copying machine. The customer can only think in terms of what you and the competition offer ... improvement is important but it is not enough. (p. 10)

A SYSTEMATIC IMPROVEMENT OF OPERATIONS

The way we currently try to improve our institutions is after the fact. We inspect outcomes rather than cause quality. Daniel Seymour refers to the process as "inspecting in" quality and admonishes us that this will never work. It is what all of the total quality gurus advise against. We must begin to cause quality, rather than review after the fact to determine if we were successful in the first place. The adage is to prevent rather than to repair. Seymour lists several standard vehicles used by universities and colleges to measure quality that fall into the "inspect in" category: accreditation processes, program reviews, standing committees, and control-minded governing boards.

The prevention of error at the source saves much time and investigation downstream. Instead of inspecting or repairing a problem at the point of receiving the service, the errors are prevented at the point of service delivery. If the data entry staff members check their work for accuracy, and prevent 20% additional errors from occurring, they save the customer the aggravation caused by receiving an inaccurate bill, and for an internal customer, save the business manager from spending valuable time investigating the error and correcting it later.

Moreover, a division of job duties allows people to lay blame when something goes wrong in the process. Consequently, the following comments may be heard: 'that wasn't my job; someone else did that piece; if only I had gotten something worth working on; they never pay attention to what they are doing; they must be idiots; can't they read?' It is important that the barriers between departments are broken down to allow for one continuous process chain, where employees view each other as customers, deserving of the best possible product every step of the way.

The improvement process is also data-driven. Rather than relying on hunches or historical data, TQM teams develop skills in data collection and analysis to illuminate the root causes of problems and to identify solutions that are meaningful to the customers.

Develop Human Resources

When dealing with staff members, the first directive of TQM is to eliminate fear. Deming and Juran both believe that the majority of problems in the delivery of a service or good is due to the inadequacy of the process, not the employees. The usual approach to problem solving is to figure out who "screwed up." Laying blame creates an atmosphere of fear where the main goal is to ensure no trail remains and no risks are taken. Deming cajoles managers to eliminate fear in order to create an environment where front line employees are trusted to provide insight and solutions for problems in the process; one can only gain from their vantage point of actually interacting with the customer. Who better will know what the customer wants and needs?

Teamwork is the emphasized work style with people crossing departmental boundaries to bring a synergy of expertise and experience to the problem-solving table. When TQM groups have diagrammed out the work processes, and discovered that no-one individual in the process chain understands all the steps in the process, it is clear that boundaries exist. Training and continuous improvement of employees is also stressed. TQM provides training for leaders of teams enabling them, in turn, to provide 'just-in-time' training for the individual team members in the use of the TQM tools.

Long-Term Thinking

Those who implement TQM must be comfortable with long-range goals. TQM is a cultural transformation, something that certainly does not occur overnight. However, small successes of pilot teams can fuel the fire of excitement and willingness of others to participate actively. Remember that it took the Japanese nearly 30 years to turn around the perception that goods produced in Japan are of high if not superior quality. Now it is almost difficult to remember that "Made in Japan" was synonymous with poor quality. Obviously, this is a long-term process and commitment.

Commitment to Quality

The commitment to Total Quality Management has to come from the top of the organization. Juran discovered that even though workers knew how to apply the concepts of continuous improvement to the analysis of their work processes, unrelenting improvement could not prevail without top level support and understanding. It also means that management must listen more and direct less often. A constructive feature of TQM is that it gives a common language to all members of the organization so the commitment is diffused orally throughout.

GETTING STARTED WITH TQM

Once a commitment is made to TQM, an implementation plan is necessary. There are several steps and tools commonly used to execute TQM. After an interdisciplinary team is formed, a critical process is selected, and customers are surveyed to provide input to the process, define quality and identify concerns about the process. Then the specific issue is selected and a goal is stated. For example, 'decrease the turnaround time on interlibrary loans.' Next, the process is plotted out on a process flow diagram. Teams have found duplicate and unnecessary steps in processes by simply effecting this one step. Once the process is mapped out, the cause of the problem is explored through brainstorming and a tool labeled a fishbone diagram. More data is collected to ensure that the cause or causes are the root problem. The data are diagramed by using additional TQM tools including histograms, pareto charts, scatter diagrams, run charts and statistical process control charts. This enables the team to avoid jumping to a conclusion that may miss the needs of the customer, or inappropriately satisfy the needs of the organization, instead of the customer. A solution is determined and implemented. The results are monitored against the original data to ascertain if the desired outcome, (recall the issue statement), is achieved.

Periodically, monitoring occurs to ensure that the root cause does not reoccur and to examine other opportunities for improvement. This is the stage where many people realize that the TQM process is not a project with an end point. Once an organization commits to TQM, they have committed to continuous improvement, where the cycle repeats itself over and over again.

The sequential approach to problem solving and continuous process improvement may take as little as a few months to as long as 18 months. The length of time from first team meeting to the implementation of a solution will be impacted by many factors including the complexity of the process being studied, the size of the team, the ability of the team to meet regularly, the duration of each meeting, the support of the team members' managers and supervisors, and the ability of the group facilitator to keep the team moving without sacrificing the attainment of consensus. Of course, there are many factors external to the TQM process that will impact the ability of the team to conduct its work, and these will vary among organizations.

TQM brings new tools and jargon to an organization. Those who are not directly involved may feel alienated or intimidated. These feelings may be shared by new team members who are getting acquainted with TQM for the first time. Therefore it is useful to become familiar with the tools and the jargon as quickly as possible and to disseminate this information throughout the organization. Daniel Seymour (1992) clearly explains several of the tools and their uses.

TOOLS FOR PROCESS IMPROVEMENT

Flow charts or process flow diagrams are the visual representation of the various steps involved in a process. A process cannot be improved unless everyone understands and agrees on what the process is. To that end, a flow chart describes what is going on.

Cause and effect or *fishbone diagrams* are used to depict (causes) of a specific problem (effect) and to group them according to categories. Brainstorming sessions, observation, interviewing, or survey research are often used to enumerate the causes.

Pareto Charts are used to separate the most important characteristics of an event from the least important characteristics of an event. It is a way to sort out the vital few from the trivial many.

Histograms are used to measure the frequency of an occurrence which then is displayed as a frequency distribution. Histograms provide valuable information concerning the variability present in a process.

Run charts show the results of a process plotted over a period of time. They are useful to see the dynamic aspects of a process and to identify cyclical patterns.

Scatter Diagrams show the relationship or association (but not the cause and effect) between any two variables.

Control charts are run charts with statistically determined upper and lower limits. They are used to study the amount of variation in a process and to make judgements about the source of that variation (p. 86-87).

CONCLUSION

Higher education is experiencing factors that typically motivate institutions to change. Competition for students, faculty and staff is increasing, costs are escalating, pressure is mounting for institutions to be accountable for positive outcomes, and customers are demanding more from a service perspective. The primary external customers are students, parents, governing boards and legislators. The internal customers are all of the employees of the organization.

As TQM prevails in other private and public sector organizations, higher education will receive increasing pressure to apply the concept of continuous improvement to the campus. It is ironic that higher education is viewed as leader in creating new ideas, yet sometimes delays implementation of these ideas. Deming himself is an academic and statistician. Yet his ideas and those of the other quality gurus have not been assimilated in higher education. It is undoubtedly time to focus internally to improve the way we serve our customers.

Some institutions have begun to implement TQM, and have experienced success in the early stages; examples include Fox Valley Technical College, Oregon State University and the North Dakota State University System. These early pioneers of TQM say that it may take three to five years to see any improvements, because this is a transformation of organization culture. Certainly, higher education has the time. In fact, the transformation is not radical from a core values perspective as the values of TQM are similar to those of higher education: people, knowledge and continuous improvement. The vital transformation is in the implementation of the values in every day practice. This requires an emphasis on the customer to define the quality aspects of the service or product, a systematic improvement of operations, the development of human resources, long-term thinking, and an organization-wide commitment to quality.

A final few words. Be kind to those who pioneer the TQM projects, keep an open mind, be flexible and be forever patient. The rewards appear to be worth it.

DEMING'S FOURTEEN POINTS

1. Create constancy of purpose for the improvement of product and service.
2. Adopt a new philosophy: we are in a new economic age. Customers will no longer stand for past levels of mistakes, delays, defective products and poor workmanship. Furthermore, increasing quality does not necessarily mean increasing cost.
3. Use modern science. Cease dependence on inspection to achieve quality. Quality cannot be inspected into a product or service.
4. End the practice of awarding business on the basis of price tag. Keep TOTAL costs in mind, not partial costs.
5. Improve constantly and forever the system of production and service, to improve quality and productivity, and thus

constantly decrease costs. Find problems. Management must work continually on the system.
6. Never stop training on the job.
7. Improve supervision of workers and managers. Institute leadership. The aim of leadership should be to help people, machines, and gadgets to do a better job.
8. Drive out fear, so everyone may work effectively for the organization.
9. Break down barriers between departments. An organization must work as a team.
10. Eliminate slogans and targets without providing means.
11. Eliminate work standards that have only numerical quotas. Substitute leadership. Eliminate management by objectives. Eliminate management by numbers and numerical goals. Substitute leadership.
12. Remove barriers that stand between the worker and his/her right to pride in workmanship.
13. Institute a vigorous program of education and self-improvement.
14. Put everybody in the organization to work to accomplish the transformation. The transformation is everybody's job (Deming, 1986).

BIBLIOGRAPHY

Bemowski, Karen "Restoring the Pillars of Higher Education," *Quality Progress*, October 1991, pp. 35-42.
Carothers, Robert L. "Trippingly on the Tongue: Translating Quality for the Academy," *AAHE Bulletin*, November 1992, pp. 6-10.
Chaffee, Ellen Earle, "TQM Workshop," a presentation for the Arizona State University Management Development Series, October 1991.
Coate, L. Edwin "Implementing Total Quality Management in a University Setting," Oregon State University, July 1990.
Crosby, Philip *Quality is Free: The Art of Making Quality Certain*, New York: Mcgraw-Hill Book Company, 1979.
Deming, W. Edwards *Out of the Crisis*, Cambridge, MA: MIT Center for Advanced Engineering Study, 1986.
Gabor, Andrea *The Man Who Discovered Quality: How W. Edwards Deming Brought the Quality Revolution to America*, New York: Random House, Inc., 1990.

Ishikawa, Kaoru *What is Total Quality Control? The Japanese Way.* Englewood Cliffs, New Jersey: Prentice-Hall, Inc., 1985. Translated by David J. Lu.

Kehoe, Dalton "TQM and the University," a presentation to the NACUBO Conference held in Toronto, Ontario Canada, July 1992.

Mangan, Katherine S. "TQM: Colleges Embrace the Concept of Total Quality Management," *The Chronicle of Higher Education*, August 12, 1992, pp. A25-26.

Marchese, Theodore J. "AAHE and TQM," *AAHE Bulletin*, November 1992, p. 11.

Seymour, Daniel T. *On Q: Causing Quality in Higher Education*, New York: American Council on Education and Macmillan Publishing Company, 1992.

Sherr, Lawrence "Quality in Higher Education," a presentation for Arizona State University's Quality and Service Excellence seminar, September 1991.

Thor, Linda "The Student as Customer: Another Kind of Accountability," *Vision*, Spring 1992, pp. 12-13.

Walton, Mary *The Deming Management Method*, New York: The Putnam Publishing Group, 1986.

Library Leadership: Does Gender Make a Difference?

Paula T. Kaufman

There are more women than ever in leadership roles, throughout society, and librarianship is no exception. More women than ever are assuming roles as leaders in librarianship, as directors of our professional organizations, as directors of our library education programs, as leaders of thought and vision, and, perhaps most notably, as directors of our libraries small and large, academic, public, and special. Ever since its founding more than a century ago, the library profession has been populated primarily by women, yet led by men. Although this is now changing, ours is still a highly feminized profession in which men continue to hold most of the leadership positions. In 1991, although 80% of the library work force consisted of women, 80% of all management positions were held by men.[1] However, during the last two decades women have made notable strides in reaching library leadership positions, and there is no reason to think that this trend will not continue.[2]

This article will examine the possible impacts and implications of female leadership on the library profession. Is gender a critical factor in effective leadership? Can we expect significant changes in the profession attributable to the rising numbers of female leaders? What are the essential qualities needed and factors that must be

---

Paula T. Kaufman is Dean of Libraries at the University of Tennessee, Knoxville, TN.

[Haworth co-indexing entry note]: "Library Leadership: Does Gender Make a Difference?" Kaufman, Paula T. Co-published simultaneously in the *Journal of Library Administration* (The Haworth Press, Inc.) Vol. 18, No. 3/4, 1993, pp. 109-128; and: *Catalysts for Change: Managing Libraries in the 1990s* (ed: Gisela M. von Dran and Jennifer Cargill) The Haworth Press, Inc., 1993, pp. 109-128. Multiple copies of this article/chapter may be purchased from The Haworth Document Delivery Center [1-800-3-HAWORTH; 9:00 a.m. - 5:00 p.m. (EST)].

© 1993 by The Haworth Press, Inc. All rights reserved.

considered to lead U.S. libraries effectively at the end of the twentieth century and into the twenty-first?

As we begin to explore the role and implications of females as library leaders, we must keep two cautions in mind. First, we must recognize that it can be dangerous to overgeneralize, as so many authors do on the subject of gender differences in leadership. It is important to remember that although women bring diversity to leadership, there is also significant diversity among women. Second, we must also recognize the inherent difficulties of trying to define leadership. As Warren Bennis says in his book *Leaders*, leadership is the most studied and least understood topic in all the social sciences. Like beauty, or love, we know it when we see it, but we have difficulty defining it easily or producing it on demand.[3]

DEMOGRAPHICS

Nearly 5.6 million women were employed as executives, administrators, and managers in the United States in 1988, more than at any other time in our history, and currently women hold about 40 percent of all executive, administrative, and managerial positions.[4] The U.S. Department of Labor estimates that the group of executive, administrative, and managerial occupations will be among the top three fastest growing major occupational groups by the year 2005, gaining nearly 3 million jobs. Women will account for 62 percent of the net growth in the labor force between 1990 and 2005, and thus can be expected to continue to occupy a growing proportion of positions in the executive, administrative, and managerial category.[5] That women will continue to emerge as leaders in all professions and industries is inevitable.

The changes experienced by women in the work force in this century are striking, but the changes experienced by men during this same period, although perhaps less apparent, are no less important. Men in different age groups and with different marital status had been employed at approximately the same rates for at least 80 years. Recently, however, men have been increasingly required to adapt to the presence of women as their peers and supervisors.[6]

Librarianship has always been a female-intensive profession, and there is no reason to think that this will change significantly. We can assume, however, that as the people who employ librarians become more enlightened, as societal pressures for equal representation, diversity, and equity increase, and as female library leaders provide good role models and mentoring opportunities, there will be increasing numbers of women who will take up leadership roles in the library profession.

The increase of females in the ranks of library leadership positions is creating a set of role models and new expectations and achievable goals for the very many women in the library profession. At the same time, however, the minority male librarian population must deal with perceptions of diminished opportunities.

MEN AND WOMEN AS LEADERS

Are men and women similar in the way in which they behave, in their personal traits, attributes, and characteristics? Or can we identify some truly fundamental differences between them, differences that will make one group or the other inherently better suited to lead the library profession, its organizations and institutions, into the complex and unknown future?

There have been numerous studies of the differences in men and women as leaders. The results of this work have been reported both in the scholarly and popular presses, and, not surprisingly, they often contradict one another. The rise of the woman's movement and the beginning of research to rationalize the lack of female leaders led to an early focus on the differences in the ways in which men and women are raised and socialized as the explanation for the paucity of successful female leaders. In *Games Mother Never Taught Me*, Harragan was the first to popularize the notion that because girls were discouraged from playing team sports, and because they were reinforced in their "traditional" female roles as wife and mother through their play they were at a disadvantage as team players and captains, managers and leaders within organizations.[7]

In his *Handbook of Leadership*, Bass observes that girls and women differ from boys and men in many attributes, and Bass contends that these differences may be reflected in the different ways in which men and women have emerged, and function, as leaders.[8] Writers such as Bass contend that men and women have different inherent characteristics. They often use such adjectives as participative, caring, and transformational to describe female leaders and such adjectives as powerful, controlling, aggressive, and transactional to describe male leaders.[9]

Social scientists often ascribe male leaders' power to the organization, to control, and to self-interest, whereas they ascribe females' power to personal characteristics such as charisma, interpersonal skills, and hard work.[10] Men are supposedly more focused on competition, winning, and domination, and are said to take more risks, to be better team players, and to be more independent, opportunistic, and impersonal than women in their working relationships. Women, on the other hand, are viewed as being better than men at giving information, strengthening interpersonal relationships, being receptive to ideas, encouraging effort and subordinate development, and at assuming supportive roles.[11]

Although these descriptions seem simplistic and naive, and although the reader will know men and women to whom each set, or part of each set, of adjectives could be well applied, this typology continues to predominate. As recently as 1990, Judith Rosener, in her *Harvard Business Review* article reporting on her study of more than 450 leaders, concluded that there is a significant difference between the sexes as leaders.[12]

Based on the mean scores of the responses of 355 female leaders and 101 males matched for position, type, and size or organization, Rosener profiled the typical female leader. The average female leader in Rosener's study does not describe herself as predominantly "feminine," "masculine," or "gender-neutral." Rather, she exhibits qualities associated with all of these sex-roles identities. However, she sees herself as more forceful, assertive, dominant, independent, and tough (masculine-associated attributes) and less submissive mild, and dependent (feminine-associated attributes) than her male peers. She also describes herself as more conscientious and efficient (gender-neutral associated attributes) than her male counterparts.[13]

In Rosener's profile, the typical female leader is a transformational one, meaning that she motivates those with whom she works by transforming individual self interests into a desire to achieve organizational goals and attain the organization's vision. She prefers the use of personal power, that is, power based on her charisma, personality, work record, and contacts, as contrasted with structural power based on the authority that comes with organizational position, title, and the ability to reward and punish.

Rosener concludes that the sex identity characteristics are apparent in male and female leaders. However, she also feels that it is possible for women to succeed as leaders in business, government, educational, and non-profit organizations without assuming "masculine" characteristics.

Ann Gregory reviewed existing literature on gender differences to determine if women are different and why women are perceived to be different. She looked at several areas: personality, motivation to manage, and leadership. She concluded that although there are few, if any, personality differences between male and female managers, the perception still exists that women lack the personality qualities important for managers. She also found that in organizations with 19% of its managers female, there was no difference in motivation to manage, while in an organization with only 6% of its managers female, women showed a lower motivation to manage. Further, she found that there are few differences in the ways in which males and females exercise leadership.[14]

In an attempt to review all of the literature on the topic, Alice Eagly and Blair Johnson recently undertook a meta-analysis of the published research on gender differences in leadership. They reasoned that organizational roles are more important than gender roles, and they predicted that differences between men and women occupying the same leadership roles in organizations would be small.[15] When social behavior is regulated by other less diffuse social roles, as it is in organizational settings, they postulated, behavior should primarily reflect the influence of these roles, and therefore lose much of its gender-stereotypic character. Their findings substantiated their hypothesis, suggesting that there are only some very small differences in the leadership styles of men and women even in organizational settings. Women behave somewhat less aggressively than men; women's leadership styles are more democratic than men's.[16]

Ann-Marie Rizzo and Carmen Mendez have analyzed and compared the results of studies based on the application of a variety of methodological approaches–trait, style and contingency studies on sex differences and leader behavior and effectiveness. They found that organizational socialization processes and long-term exposure to female managers appears to erode sex stereotyped attitudes. They concluded from their analysis that women use fundamentally the same personal influence strategies as male leaders to influence others in a work organization. They also found that assertive behavioral strategies remain one of the few characteristics distinguishing males from females.[17]

It is important to examine whether there are perceived differences between males and females as leaders, and, if so, whether these perceived differences influence effectiveness. Sarla Murgai studied attitudes of library and information science students toward female library leaders. The vast majority of respondents felt that women were as capable as men of being good leaders. Except for the variable of aggressiveness, women and men were perceived to be remarkably similar.[18]

Are women and men different as leaders? Although some authors contend that they are, the research evidence as analyzed by Gregory, Eagly and Johnson, and Rizzo and Mendez, suggests that although the two genders may differ in some small ways and at some times, the differences are minimal and insignificant. There may be some perceived differences between the capacity of males and females to be effective leaders, but these appear to be relatively insignificant. If male and female leadership characteristics are basically indistinguishable, can we expect any changes in the library profession as females assume more leadership roles?

LEADERSHIP

If males and females do not possess significantly different traits that make one gender inherently better able to be effective leaders, what then are the characteristics and behaviors that any library leader must possess, both today and in the future? Clearly, there is no formula that magically produces a leader, in librarianship or in any other occupation or profession. Good leadership skills are by their very nature indefinable. However, after years of study by researchers, there are some useful generalizations we can make to characterize effective leaders. Before exploring this issue, however, it is important to have a clear understanding of the difference between leaders and managers.

A recent study of high-level executives categorized respondents as having either a "leader style" or a "manager style." These descriptions are a useful shorthand for differentiating between leaders and managers. The report depicts leaders as visionary, innovative, and strategic in their thinking. Managers, on the other hand, are portrayed as concerned with maintaining momentum, balancing interests, stabilizing forces, and implementing tactical plans.[19] Leadership produces movement whereas management produces a degree of consistency. Leaders think long-range and understand instinctively the complexities and ambiguities within which the organization operates currently and within which it will operate in the future. Managers, on the other hand, tend to accept the organizational structure and processes as they are.[20]

There have been many studies, comments, and observations about leadership, and they are often in agreement about very little. However, the one factor about which they all agree, the one thing that is the core essence of leadership, is that a leader shapes and shares a vision that gives meaning and point to the work of others. Although there is much more than this required for effective leadership, one cannot lead effectively without a driving vision.

Having a vision that gives meaning to the work of others differentiates leaders from others. Charles Handy, British philosopher and a leading observer of leadership, identifies five principles evident in the work of successful leaders. First, the leader's vision must be different. A vision has to "reframe" the known, reconceptualize the obvious, connect the previously unconnected dream. The vision must be transformational, not merely transactional. Second, the vision must make sense to others. It should create the "Aha Effect." ("Aha, of course, now I see it. Why didn't I think of that?") It must stretch people's imaginations and, to give meaning to the work of others, it must be related to their work and not to some grand design in which they feel they have no stake. Third, the vision must be understandable. It has to be a vision that sticks in the mind. Fourth, leaders must live the vision. They must not only believe in it but they must be seen to believe in it. It must come from within their deepest soul, from an inner system of belief. "The total pragmatist cannot be a transforming leader." Finally, the leader must remember that it is the work of others without which the vision is only a dream. "A leader with no followers is a voice in the wilderness."[21]

The best leaders, most agree, deal with our mercurial world by anticipating, looking not just down the road but around the corner, by seeing opportunities rather than obstacles, and by embracing change instead of resisting it. Warren Bennis, who has written extensively on the subject, says that a leader "stands tall and leans out, taking charge of her own course, with a clear view of where she's going."[22] Leaders take risks to reach their vision of the future, to bring about changes, to influence the quality and direction of the organization. As leaders seek to attain their vision for the organization, however, they do not necessarily focus solely on the future at the expense of the past. Good leaders embrace the very best of the organization's history, traditions, and values without enshrining the past for its own sake.[23]

To reach their visions, to bring about the changes necessary for their organizations, leaders are willing to risk their own careers, to risk criticism from colleagues when articulating their vision. But, more importantly, individuals who emerge as leaders are prepared to act on their own visions. Much of their action takes place in a realm of ambiguity, that world which encircles most of our modern institutions.

In a world filled with ambiguity and complexity, only those organizations steered by effective leaders will reach a steady course for the future, although effective leaders will change course, and will change their visions when appropriate. Visionary, risk-taking, change-embracing, flexible–all describe the very best leaders who will make it through the stormy seas of our modern age. None of these descriptors are gender-specific, and none of them implies that one gender is better suited for leadership than the other.

Not all visions turn out as well as leaders had planned or hoped. Some are derailed by unforeseen events, some are short-sighted, and some are just plain wrong. And, some are poorly implemented. Visionary leaders, effective leaders, must be flexible and exercise what Burt Nanus describes as "prudence": monitoring change, making necessary corrections, and knowing when to start a new vision-forming process.[24]

Leaders have vision and they take risks, but they cannot act alone. Leaders of organizations are leaders of people, and it is with people that leaders reach the end-states they envision for their organizations. Although leaders are willing to risk criticism from their colleagues, they cannot achieve change without the help of their colleagues. Leaders need their colleagues not only to help reach their visions of the future, but they also need and want their colleagues to help shape those visions, to contribute their ideas, to criticize what they see, to help form and shape and sharpen the vision, to make the vision happen, to give meaning and point to their work. It is through this process that leaders develop their colleagues' emotional commitment and buy-into the goals of the organization so they will help plan and develop the strategies, tactics, and actions required to attain them.[25]

Successful leadership depends on other people and successful leaders recognize that people are an organization's most vital asset. Leaders who nurture their staff's talents, who encourage new ideas, who build trust among their employees, who share information, who blend and combine and interact with care and understanding will have the most success in bringing about the changes they desire with the least disruption to an organization's equilibrium and stability.

Leaders have vision, take risks, effect change, by working with people, by generating and sustaining trust, by caring about their employees, and by nurturing them and their talents. Warren Bennis identifies four characteristics displayed by all successful leaders as they do this.

- *Constancy*—Leaders cannot create surprises for their employees regardless of the surprises they must face themselves. Successful leaders "stay the course."
- *Congruity*—Leaders "walk their talk." Leaders must practice the theories they espouse.
- *Reliability*—Good leaders are always there when it counts. They are prepared to support their colleagues in the moments that matter.

- *Integrity*—Leaders always honor their promises and commitments.[26]

To harness their power, leaders must share their visions, inspire commitment. Power can come from many sources. Often, power derives from a position itself, but the successful leader understands that positional power itself is insufficient, and positional power alone is ineffective. Empowering people by sharing authority, by recognizing that power also derives from knowledge and skill, makes leaders successful. Sharing visions and sharing power are equally important.

Leaders most frequently occupy a position of leadership (e.g., the director's office), but they are not limited to this position. Good leaders may be found anywhere and everywhere, for they do not just spring full-blown as directors. They may hold any position in a library and may use a variety of strategies with which to exert their leadership. Within the library profession, leaders occupy any number of positions. Leaders in professional organizations, for example, are not necessarily library directors, and all library directors are not necessarily leaders. Effective library leaders will also exert their leadership within the larger organizations that encompass their libraries.

As we have seen, good leaders possess vision, integrity, courage, judgment, understanding of others, optimism, and flexibility. Leadership is moving people to change, moving people to share one's visions and dreams, to trust in one's leadership and to embrace the future together. Successful leaders paint their visions so brightly and articulately, with such conviction and enthusiasm, that their colleagues will share the dream. Colleagues who are empowered to act on those shared visions will change the organization so the visions are reached. Leaders are men and women who lead people. People lead and manage organizations.

CHANGING MODELS OF ORGANIZATIONS

Will the influx of women leaders in librarianship have any impact on our library organizations? Are the changing organizational models better suited for female leaders, even though the differences between females and males leaders are very small?

Theories of management and organizational leadership have evolved over the last century since the emergence of Taylor's theories of scientific management and since Max Weber's ideals of bureaucracy became associated with rigidity and control. Until only a few years ago, most successful organizations were described in terms of structure and systems. Libraries were no exception. Hierarchical, bureaucratic structures helped libraries to insure accuracy and attain stability in the performance of the many routine processes and systems that form their core.

But today, pyramid-shaped bureaucracies, imbued with values borrowed from the military, in which orders are accepted without question and in which there are fixed hierarchies of positions, in which tradition is sufficient reason to continue a practice and in which there is a rigid set of disciplinary controls, are being challenged and changed. Pressed by competition and fast-changing technologies, complex organizations, including libraries, are casting aside many of their old values, reducing and eliminating their hierarchical structures, and modifying some of the bureaucratic systems that now get in the way of effectiveness and creativity. The world is moving and changing much too quickly for the old "lone hero" to reign at the top of a pyramid. Today, that lone hero has been, for the most part, stranded and will be ultimately abandoned, replaced by people working collaboratively and more autonomously.[27]

Old models, however, are old indeed, and they have changed not because women began to play influential roles in organizations but instead because it was recognized that traditional bureaucracies, imbued with control and conformity, in which workers were viewed as just one of the organization's many expendable resources, were ineffective in meeting the demands of our changing global society. Researchers, typified by Irving Janis, have demonstrated that the domination of any organizational group by one or two members, such as in the typical hierarchical, bureaucratic models, leads by the pressure to conform to premature consensus and poor decisions.[28] Bureaucracies produce feelings of alienation. Today, we need our organizations to bridge the gap between the demands of efficiency and the need to nurture the most important of the organization's assets–its human employees. Our organizations need a new breed of leader of either gender.

Some authors believe that the 1990s may witness the beginning of the end of the traditional organization.[29] A century dominated by bureaucracy is giving way to a new era of organizational structure, although it is difficult today to tell exactly where we are in the transition to a new organizational paradigm or paradigms. It is useful, however, to explore briefly some of the "look and feel" of future organizations.

It is inevitable that libraries exist in networks of suppliers, and users. Organizational boundaries will become fuzzy as libraries forge a variety of alliances, both with other libraries and with suppliers and users. These blurry organizational boundaries will be the result of strategic intent and design, and will be constructed with thought and skill. Library leaders will have the critical role of defining boundaries to be consistent with strategy in any area of service. The days of rigid boundaries, are today ending as new forms of interorganizational collaboration emerge.

Future library organizations will be fluid and transitory. Each will look different, but many will feature collaboration and teams that will be able to shift constantly as a result of changing conditions and needs. With large numbers of teams doing the work, values rather than rules and direct supervision will furnish the cohesion necessary to provide direction and achieve coordination. It will become increasingly important for leaders to shape the vision and values of the organization and to spend an increasing amount of time and energy focusing on the development of people.

There is little argument that it is time to change the old organizational models. The global economy and information society are changing the rules and introducing some new ones. What is emerging today is an emphasis by organizational leaders on a more productive and more human workplace, an emphasis on a workplace that is driven by the needs of customers and users, and a workplace that meets the needs of its workers.

As we have seen, today's effective leaders concentrate on bringing about change in their colleagues through individual growth, not through collusion and coercion. Today's leaders must be tireless advocates with a vitalizing mission, with a vision of the future they can attain in collaboration with a committed and dedicated staff.

Gilbert Fairholm describes a new leadership model, values leadership, that may have particular applicability to libraries because of its focus on service and concern for users. The values model of leadership is a way to think about and value the leadership process, leaders who practice it, and the followers who are affected by it. Values leadership views leadership as a new mind-set, as a philosophy and a way of leading more than a theory or technique. Values leadership stresses operationalizing a people-oriented philosophy of growth toward self-leadership.[30]

> The distinction between new leadership models and past models is not in the fact that they have a values focus, but in the particular value set espoused by each. Values leadership is founded on this different-values base. It has emerged as both a new leader technology and a set of guiding principles of action. It has a special technology that focuses on ideas like innovation, concern for customers, quality, and simple structure. Values leadership is also a new orientation governing the leader's role. Its principles include those of service to others, individual development and growth, and self-determination. Values leadership also has a strategic focus and prioritizes excellent performance.

The emerging model of values leadership does not focus on leader traits of personality, on behavioral patterns, or on critical contingencies. Rather, it focuses on the relationships engaged in, the attitudes that underlie those relationships, and the philosophy or mind-set the leader adopts. Its central orientation is on a philosophy of leadership, or on what leaders think and value about leadership.[31]

Values are broad general beliefs about the way people should behave, or about some end state they should attain. They are conclusive beliefs individuals develop gradually about what is true or right or good about their world. People form their values in the same way in which they develop their personality. Values come from early conditioning, experience, and significant events in one's life. Values are criteria for selecting actions, goals, and methods. Some values are explicit, others are not. They nonetheless trigger some specific behavior and constrain behavior that contravenes the values.

Organizations have values, too. They are often codified in mission or vision statements, and they provide the infrastructure for transmitting and implementing specific behavior towards specific goals and results. These values are powerful in shaping group member behavior and in validating institutional policy and mission. They determine acceptable actions, resolve conflicts, determine sanctions systems employed, and are integral to reward systems.[32]

Clearly, today's organizations must be transformed if they are to be successful in the future, and organizations and leaders without appropriate values will not prosper. Society is being transformed from the dominator to the partnership model, and to a values-based model. Organizational cultures are also being transformed to a gentler, or in terms of stereotypes, to a more "feminine" style of leadership. Some authors suggest that the nurturing management behaviors shown by new library directors, regardless of gender, suggest that women are influencing and changing the library workplace rather than adopting the stereotypical male role model.[33] There is no real evidence, however, to support the thesis that women make better leaders than men, for as we have seen, there is very little evidence that they do. The realities of our changing society require new leadership styles and approaches–and constant leadership values. These new styles can and will be applied equally well or poorly by leaders of either gender.

The nature of our information society requires leaders who care, who can make decisions, who live and radiate their values, and who communicate effectively, disseminating their visions, sharing information, listening to their colleagues who will help shape and implement their visions. "Communication is what defines the style of leadership that reconciles efficiency with human values."[34]

A new group of scholars has emerged in the 1990s, prepared to describe new approaches to leading organizations. They have conceptualized several new approaches that might serve as future models for libraries.

"The Learning Organization" is a conceptual framework in which learning is central to success. Management needs to see the big picture, to escape linear thinking, and to understand subtle interrelationships. "Reengineering" is a fundamental rethinking and redesign of an organizational system. Its proponents urge an overhaul of job designs, organizational structures, and management systems and an organization of work around outcomes, not tasks or functions.

"Core Competencies" is a strategy in which organizations identify and organize around what they do best. "Organizational Architecture" is a metaphor that forces managers to think more broadly about organization in terms of how work, people, and formal and informal structures fit together. It leads to autonomous work teams and strategic alliances. In "Time-Based Competition" the belief is that time is the equivalent of money, productivity, quality, and innovation. Proponents argue that time, like costs, is manageable and a source of competitive advantage throughout every process in the organization.[35]

These new models share several common elements. Like the leaders described above, the new models shun incremental change, they are bold in their thinking. Leaders are urged to think in radical terms. The new models also stress that smaller is better than larger and that organizations should be organized on the basis of process or outcome instead of function. They also agree that self-managed teams provide more challenge and meaning in work. Unlike the old models in which the focus was on the leader, new models urge that leaders empower their workers. Power, knowledge, information, and rewards must be moved downward in the organization.

Today's libraries cannot operate effectively without the intelligence, commitment, and enthusiasm of its employees. They are absolutely critical to success. Libraries require employees who can think, speak up, take initiative, and develop new ideas, who can and will challenge their managers and leaders.

Because most libraries operate within the context of larger organizations themselves, library leaders must play multiple leadership roles–in their libraries, in their larger organizations, and in their profession. The vestiges of old bureaucracies continue to linger, to haunt one's past and threaten to stifle environments that are undergoing at least partial transformation. Library leaders must continue to find new ways to lead, new ways to gain employee commitment and enthusiasm despite such restrictions and obstacles as salary freezes, layoffs, budget reductions, and complex institutional procedures and policies. Library leaders will emerge and lead despite the strictures of their parent organizations.

New organizations call for new thinking and new behavior, new values. Leaders must nurture their employees, encourage and empower them, give them the latitude to work in their own way, to do their own thing. The recent success of General Motors' new Saturn plant in Tennessee may be a good example of the force of empowerment and teamwork, of making a team of workers totally responsible for certain activities and operations. Although there is yet no hard evidence that there is a correlation between Saturn's new mode of operating and the success of its products in the marketplace, Saturn's leaders, by focusing on the value of the worker, on the responsibility and capability of workers, are hoping to fulfill their vision–an American-made auto that competes successfully on all counts with foreign autos, and a workforce that is committed and enthusiastic about being the reason for their company's success. Saturn's leaders' visions have given point to their workers' work. In contrast, the old models of car manufacturers conjure up images of disaffected auto workers on old assembly lines, assembly lines in which each worker was just another piece of machinery, no more or less valuable than a lathe, waiting to be replaced by a robotic counterpart.

Implementing values leadership, effecting the results that one wants, empowering workers, does not happen with the snap of a finger or the issuance of a memo. Today's leaders must share their visions of the organization and move its people from believing to doing to being. This role is radically different from directing, planning, and controlling–major elements of old models of leadership. This new role involves enlarging group members' perceptions, getting them to explore the possibilities of the situation, helping them to embrace change instead of resisting it, urging them to consider one's ideas and improve upon them. Leaders must draw out individuals and raise their abilities and capabilities to perform. Leaders must be able to lead people who know as much or more about the details of the organization than they do, who are the subject and technical experts, the people who will implement and operationalize their visions. Leaders have an integrating perspective, and their tasks will in the future be one of integrating disparate experts. As our organizations become more complex and multi-differentiated, leaders must find ways to integrate an explosion of expertise. And, leaders must create an organizational climate that encourages a basic set of values and attitudes that encourage creativity and that encourage results.

Clearly, leaders are different from the other group members. A part of the difference leaders project is high energy and enthusiastic involvement. They trigger similar actions in their followers. Leaders set an emotional tone that creates the feeling that their shared goals are attainable. Leaders spend less time on day-to-day problem solving and more on imagining and simulating a future no one has yet experienced. Tomorrow's library leaders will most likely be spending their time in dealing with new problems, in creative and innovative activity, not in routine managerial activities.

LIBRARY LEADERSHIP FOR THE FUTURE

Tomorrow's library leaders may come from anywhere. Being male will be neither an advantage nor a disadvantage. Being female will be neither an advantage nor a disadvantage. It is highly likely that the traditional paths that led to the top of pyramid-shaped libraries will be dead ends in the future. Leaders will emerge because they are leaders for tomorrow, able to cope with complexity, diversity, and change the trends of the next century.

Today's library organizations are still primarily pyramid-shaped hierarchies, imbued with the traditional values of traditional bureaucracies. Such organizations do not necessarily respond well to a highly dynamic and changing environment. In order to provide a climate that will encourage and nourish innovation and creativity, library leaders must look for ways to provide more flexibility. Changes in the structures of many library organizations will cause them to look considerably different tomorrow as leaders change their structures, processes, and systems, and the ways in which they do their business. To operate successfully in the future, libraries must nurture leadership at all levels, and the number and complexity of levels must be reduced. "Leadership should not rest solely with the director of the library or the administrative and managerial group, though these individuals have a clear mandate to provide leadership."[36] Individuals will continue to lead libraries.

Libraries do not differ significantly from other organizations, and the characteristics of library leaders closely resemble those of leaders in other fields. The path to leadership roles is demanding, intense, and cluttered with barriers, and few people of either gender will succeed. There are no data that indicate that the gender of library leaders will make an iota of difference in their effectiveness. However, there is much food for thought about how library leaders' effectiveness can be enhanced.

CONCLUSION

Leadership is clear yet hard to define. There are no magic formulas, no secret recipes to ensure success. The question in the 1990s is no longer whether men and women possess the same individual traits identified as needed for effective leadership. Rather, the question is one of how each individual in possession of these attributes chooses to order and apply them.

We are left with little reason to believe that either female leaders or male leaders are superior in executing, involving themselves in, or personally coping with the responsibilities of their jobs. The only meaningful difference between men and women may be in the environments in which they operate, with imbalanced sex ratios contributing to stereotype-driven perceptions and unrealistic expectations for women. The stereotype that men make better leaders is simply not true.

Tomorrow's leaders require qualities that are part inspiration, part gentle persuasion. Tomorrow's leaders will win commitment by setting a standard of excellence, by caring, being ethical, open, empowering, and inspiring, by being gentler and kinder, by imbuing the organization with values. When changes are made, great leaders are found in the thick of things on the playing field, not on the sidelines. Great leaders are those people who see the future and seize the moment.

NOTES

1. Sarla R. Murgai, "Attitudes Toward Women as Managers in Library and Information Science." *Sex Roles*, 24, 1991, p. 681.
2. See Marcia J. Myers and Paula T. Kaufman, "ARL Directors: Two Decades of Changes." *College & Research Libraries*, 52, May 1991, pp. 241-254 as an example.

3. Charles Handy, *The Age of Unreason*. (Boston: Harvard Business School Press, 1989).

4. U.S. Department of Labor, Women's Bureau. "Women Workers: Outlook to 2005." *Facts on Working Women*, 92-1, January 1992, p. 4.

5. *Ibid.*, pp. 1, 5.

6. Gary N. Powell, *Women & Men in Management* (Newbury Park, CA: Sage Publications, 1988), p. 39-40.

7. Betty L. Harragan, *Games Mother Never Taught You: Corporate Gamesmanship for Women* (NY: Rawson Associates, 1977).

8. Bernard M. Bass, editor, *Bass & Stogdill's Handbook of Leadership: Theory, Research, and Managerial Applications*, 3rd edition. (NY: The Free Press, 1990).

9. Judy B. Rosener, "Ways Women Lead." *Harvard Business Review*, November-December 1990, p. 120.

10. *Ibid.*, 120.

11. Rita Mae Kelly, *The Gendered Economy: Work, Careers, and Success* (Newbury Park, CA: Sage Publications, 1991).

12. Rosener, *Harvard Business Review, op. cit.*

13. Judy B. Rosener et al., *Leadership Study, International Women's Forum* (Irvine, CA: University of California, Irvine Graduate School of Management, July 1990).

14. Ann Gregory, "Are Women Different and Why are Women Thought to be Different? Theoretical and Methodological Perspectives." *Journal of Business Ethics*, 9, April/May 1990, p. 259.

15. Alice H. Eagly and Blair T. Johnson, "Gender and Leadership Style: A Meta-Analysis." *Psychological Bulletin*, 108, 1990, p. 236.

16. *Ibid.*, p. 248-249.

17. Ann-Marie Rizzo and Carmen Mendez, "Making Things Happen in Organizations: Does Gender Make a Difference?" *Public Personnel Management*, 17, Spring 1988.

18. Murgai, *op. cit.*, pp. 694-695.

19. Sharon Nelten, "Men, Women & Leadership." *Nation's Business*, 79, May 1991, p. 18.

20. *Ibid.*, p. 18.

21. Handy, *op. cit.*, pp. 124-126.

22. Michele Morris, "The New Breed of Leaders: Taking Charge in a Different Way." *Working Woman*, March 1990, p. 78.

23. Sheila D. Creth, "Organizational Leadership: Challenges Within the Library," in Anne Woodsworth and Barbara von Wahlde, editors, *Leadership for Research Libraries: Festschrift for Robert M. Hayes* (Metuchen, NJ: The Scarecrow Press, 1988), p. 81.

24. Burt Nanus, "Visionary Leadership: How to Re-Vision the Future." *The Futurist*, 26, September-October 1992, p. 23.

25. Creth, *op. cit.*, p. 81.

26. Morris, *op. cit.*, p. 76.

27. Sally Helgesen, *The Female Advantage: Women's Ways of Leadership* (NY: Doubleday, 1990) p. 240.

28. Robert Burgin and Patsy Hansel, "Library Management: A Dialogue." *Wilson Library Bulletin*, March 1992, p. 57.

29. Marc S. Gerstein and Robert B. Shaw, "Organizational Architectures for the Twenty-First Century," in David A. Nadler et al., *Organizational Architecture: Designs for Changing Organizations.* (San Francisco: Jossey-Bass, 1992), p. 263.

30. Gilbert W. Fairholm, *Values Leadership: Toward a New Philosophy of Leadership.* (NY: Praeger, 1991), p. 53.

31. *Ibid.*, p. 56.

32. *Ibid.*, p. 66.

33. Joy M. Greiner, "A Comparative Study of the Management Styles and Career Progression Patterns of Recently Appointed Male and Female Public Library Administrators (1983-1987)." *Advances in Library Administration and Organization*, 7, 1988, p. 17.

34. Helgesen, *op. cit.*, p. 242.

35. John A. Byrne, "Management's New Gurus." *Business Week*, number 3281, August 31, 1992, p. 45.

36. Creth, *op. cit.*, p. 98.

Organizational Change in Research Libraries

Susan Lee

Organizations have been able to adapt themselves to slow changes in their environments by making small concessions to pressures, and through the import of new personnel and the diffusion of new ideas. Through these unstructured, untutored, and unconscious adaptive responses organizations have "tracked" changes in their environment(s), much as the rear wheel of a long trailer tracks the changes in direction at the front. But such natural processes are no longer appropriate when the environment changes rapidly.[1]

Today, research libraries exist in such an environment. Today's research libraries face changes occurring at rates exceeding the scope of natural assimilation processes, and lack sufficiently comprehensive methods for adjusting and adapting to the turbulence. To enhance effectiveness, achieve excellence, and ensure survival research library leaders need, in full collaboration with staff members, to develop conscious, explicit processes for organizational change.

While technological change has been continuing exponentially for the last two hundred years, it has now reached a level of pervasiveness and frequency unique to our times. No established institu-

---

Susan Lee is Associate Librarian of Harvard College for Administrative Services, Cambridge, MA.

[Haworth co-indexing entry note]: "Organizational Change in Research Libraries." Lee, Susan. Co-published simultaneously in the *Journal of Library Administration* (The Haworth Press, Inc.) Vol. 18, No. 3/4, 1993, pp. 129-143; and: *Catalysts for Change: Managing Libraries in the 1990s* (ed: Gisela M. von Dran and Jennifer Cargill) The Haworth Press, Inc., 1993, pp. 129-143. Multiple copies of this article/chapter may be purchased from The Haworth Document Delivery Center [1-800-3-HAWORTH; 9:00 a.m. - 5:00 p.m. (EST)].

© 1993 by The Haworth Press, Inc. All rights reserved.

tion in our society now perceives itself as adequate to the challenges that face it.[2] Our research libraries have virtually no historic precedent, collective experience, or policy directive to guide them through these "white water" times. We can less and less depend on our inherited organizational values and forms.

In the past we have sought to come to grips with these problems through bureaucracies which are memorials to old problems. In this, our very successes are part of what now makes us inadequate. Our old bureaucracies impede flexible response to still newer problems. And while our research libraries are now asking what new missions are appropriate, *we must go beyond defining our role in society to redefining our organization for carrying out that role.*

We must confront the phenomenon of change directly both at the level of the individual and of the organization. In the face of changes imperfectly understood, we must invent and bring into being new or modified organizational forms capable of confronting these challenges without freezing and without flying apart at the seams. And we must become capable not only of transforming our institutions, in response to changing situations and requirements; we must invent and develop institutions which are capable of bringing about their own continuing transformation. To do this, today's managers must develop an understanding of the assumptions, premises, philosophical postulates, intuitive insights, and logic of organizational development.

As defined by Bennis,[3] organizational development is "a response to change, a complex educational strategy intended to change the beliefs, attitudes, values, and structure of organizations so that they can better adapt to new technologies, markets and challenges, and the dizzying rate of change itself."

Organizational Development implies that an organization's culture should be changed to include openness, problem-solving, and innovation. And given the trend within higher education toward "doing more with less" organizational development's emphasis on tough-minded, efficient management within a context of human concerns and values can be a useful means of addressing shrinking resources.[4]

The rate of change in technology, economic reality, patterns of scholarship, and in the publishing industry and in teaching and research is pushing research libraries to redefine themselves. Acknowledging this, one of our major emphases must be on the programs needed to help other organizational processes respond more smoothly and effectively to continuous rapid change. Positive adaptation to change must become the hallmark of research libraries. Whether this will be so or not will depend in large part on the kind of organization we develop.

RAISING THE LEVEL OF GENERALITY

Traditionally, the classic research library has been organized around our basic product, the book. As organizations in the "book and journal" business, we have had to have within our libraries staff who understand the technology of books. And following this tradition, such staff came to dominate our organizations. Within the classic research library, divisions have formed around functions like acquisitions, cataloging, processing, shelving, etc. The typical research library has formed an organizational pyramid with functional units under the control of functional managers and functional managers under the control of top management.

However, just as business firms have raised the level of generality at which they define their products, with "shoe" companies saying they are in the "footwear" business and oil companies, "energy," so our research libraries must think of themselves as being in the "information" business.[5] This change must be more than nominal. It must reflect a genuine broadening of the base. We must be able to give up the old "book" mentality built on the technology of the printing press. Our charter for innovation is far broader than newer and better varieties of books.

The institution cross-section of a research library will reveal a design for addressing the functions which have been thought basic to our mission like acquisitions and cataloging. But over time the problems have shifted causing mismatches between the organizational design and the problems thought worth solving. There have always been mismatches but with the rapid rate of change, this condition of mismatch has become endemic and universal. Only by moving beyond the concepts of our established functional-based organizations will we reach a level of aggregation broad enough to allow us to see options that match the scope of our vision.

The general rule in research libraries has been that libraries, departments, and committees come into being and assume their form in response to specific problems. When the problems and crises disappear or change drastically in nature, the old organizational structure persists. Because in research libraries as in most other established institutions, the "organizational equivalent of biological death is missing,"[6] we must find new ways of adapting flexibly to the emergence of new problems and ways of discarding old structures as they become inappropriate and vestigial. We must find new ways of using personnel and allocating resources to suit new tasks as they arise.

The importance of this is not that it urges once-and-for-all redesign of our libraries, but that it *calls for continual redesign of organizational elements*. It stresses the need for an internal organization which can be continually redesigned. Under conditions of constant change, attention must focus on the process of continuous transformation. Internal restructuring should come to be seen not as an aberration but as the norm. Then and only then will the emotion and energy which previously went into the maintenance of a stable structure be invested in the process of transformation.[7]

It still remains essential for our libraries to give their members security. Individuals must have a sense of their role and identity. In order to accommodate this, there must be a shift upward in the level at which the library provides security and identity for its members. The sense of membership must move from specific elements in the organization to broad based identification with the library as a whole. A shared philosophy, a sense of unity, and an identification with the whole will facilitate change and will allow letting go of the past.

AN ARRAY OF INTEGRATIVE VEHICLES

An important foundation for responsive change is the crossing of boundaries, the ability to seek and tie together diverse sources of data and experience. More and more the structures that will help research libraries solve problems will be cross-divisional and cross-functional involving coordinating mechanisms for exchange or expertise across areas. A hallmark of research libraries that are change oriented will be a large number of integrative mechanisms encouraging fluidity of boundaries. Staff will have multiple ties and relationships will crisscross the organization chart.

In the past when demands and activities were predictable, our functional specialization has been an excellent strategy. But today more than ever, it should be a priority to move beyond the traditional functional divisions and to work through cross-organizational coalitions and teams. Today each manager functions in a complex network of vertical, horizontal, and diagonal relationships, and his/her success in achieving intended objectives is often dependent upon the communication, cooperation, and support of other managers.

For our ongoing operations we will continue to need a clear structure, organization charts that show a differentiation into departments or functional units, clear reporting relationships, and specific jobs. But for more and more problems, the additional connection between and across units becomes essential: executive teams considering decisions together; dotted line reporting relationships; multidisciplinary project teams; regular meetings of councils representing several areas; crosscutting task forces; teams pulling together; and networks of peers who exchange information and support each other's projects.

Integrative, participative mechanisms do not replace the differentiation of definable segments that carry out clear and limited tasks; they supplement it. This is the concept of a second organization, *a parallel or shadow organization that links the separate units of the maintenance-oriented organization in flexible shifting ways to solve problems and guide changes.* There continues to be a clear structure for routine operations, but the predictable routine is punctuated by episodes of high involvement in change efforts and overlaid with an array of integrative vehicles.[8]

ORGANIZATIONAL CULTURE/VALUES

Research libraries must emphasize those values which are supportive of the kind of organization we are trying to build. Our success in the long run will require facilitating the assimilation of a new culture with the cornerstones of integration, collaboration, trust and innovation. To begin this process we must examine the status quo, identify priority areas where change is needed, and develop near and long term change programs. Areas that need to be reviewed include:

- organizational norms
- management of change
- organizational communication
- organizational problem solving
- team building
- overcoming resistance to change
- organizational human relations

We must examine our existing organizational culture and the ways it facilitates or hinders change. Areas which will require particular attention in the context of change include conflict resolution, negotiation, sharing different perspectives and the overarching issues of trust and innovation.

At the base of the Organizational Development movement lie fundamental value orientations. Valued organizational development goals include individual growth and increased organizational effectiveness with the capacity for self-renewal. Valued processes for reaching these goals include open communications, collaboration and the movement toward participatory power sharing.[9] Fundamentally, the Organizational Development movement promotes these values because organizational development believes that they result in effective organizational performance and personal growth.

A POLITICAL PERSPECTIVE

Change strategies inevitably affect organizational politics and in turn are affected by them. Despite this, the recognition and use of organizational politics by library managers has been cautious and conservative. At present the interest library managers display in organizational politics remains largely peripheral. Some are cautious for fear that increased political involvement will necessarily divert attention from their primary mission and somehow subvert their motives and values.

In terms relevant to organizational change, organizational politics can be defined as the use of power to modify or to protect the status quo of an organization's resource distribution system.[10] As seen in this light, organizational politics per se is neither good nor bad. Actually organizational politics can either help or hinder the library, depending on the processes used and the objectives sought. Understanding the sources, locations, and flow of power through the organization will help in two ways: determining how support can be generated within the political system to aid the work of the change program and determining what modifications to the change program would facilitate the development of effective political support.

Because of the interactive nature of organizations, any successful major change program will require complementary and supportive political changes. Collaboration requires that power be exchanged, shared, and pooled. Thus, if we want to achieve collaboration and participation, supportive political changes must occur to allow it. Some of these changes include the general reduction of power differentials between members of the staff, the transfer of power to those who are to participate in decision making, and the removal of structural obstacles to the flow of power in the organization generally and between levels of authority in particular.

The issue of participation raises the basic political issue of who should be given the right, and thus the power, to participate in decision making. The value component of organizational development by supporting the individual as a potential resource in problem solving justifies the political necessity of transferring some measure of participatory power to the staff member. Thus, although managers may not fully realize it, when they promote an organizational development program, they are provoking as well some of the political changes needed to support their program goals.

Historically, one of organizational development's principal concerns has been with leadership style.[11] In terms of organizational change, organizational development has recognized that changes on one level require complementary and reinforcing changes in organizational levels above and below that level.[12] It is not surprising then to see that organizational development has developed a value based view of leader/subordinate relations that supports the power exchange required for collaboration and interlevel adjustments between staff and managers. The fact that organizational development values participation, collaboration, and the upward flow of influence produces complementary and reinforcing political changes.

The move toward the use of cross-functional coalitions and teams facilitates problem solving and communications. Such integrative mechanisms by encouraging fluidity of boundaries, promote a range of political changes. The complex network of vertical, horizontal and diagonal relationships with its exchange of expertise across areas blurs authority and shifts power bases. Again these political changes can reinforce the organizational change efforts.

Library managers who understand *the relationship between the values underlying organizational development and related political changes* will be better positioned to ensure that the planned changes are successfully implemented. Broader recognition of Organizational Development's political orientations and the further development of political skills and knowledge are needed. A manager who can skillfully act as a political facilitator can establish a political climate that is supportive of the planned changes. The effectiveness of change programs can be enhanced when managers recognize, accept, and use a political orientation in the service of organizational change.

STRATEGIC ORGANIZATIONAL CHANGE REPLACES STRATEGIC PLANNING

In the hierarchy of research libraries, top management has seen its key role as planning, first defining planned changes and then taking responsibility for spreading those changes to the rest of the organization. Traditionally this has been done through long range planning efforts, the provision of resources, training and instruction, and regulation. And because our research libraries have taken as a given our particular technology and the demand for our product, planning has focused primarily on improving our technological systems associated with books and journals.

But because we live in a state of continuous change, goals established today may become obsolete tomorrow. In today's environment centralized formal planning that is approached as a long term intervention often lags behind real issues. In today's environment we need a different kind of response from top management. Management's focus should be on designing and bringing into being the institutional processes through which new problems can continually be confronted and old structures continually discarded. One of the major emphases in any planning effort must be on the programs needed to help other organizational process respond more smoothly and effectively to continuous rapid change.

Implicit in this thinking is a negative judgement about the feasibility of long-term forecasting. Attentiveness to the problems confronting research libraries can express itself either in a desire to predict future problems in order to design policies and programs for them ahead of time, or in attempts to make our research libraries increasingly flexible and responsive to the changing requirements we are unable to anticipate. Strategically planned development of the capacity for quick, flexible response must be substituted for our traditional long range planning efforts to predict accurately what lies ahead. The era of static strategic planning may be over; we are entering an era of constant replanning focused on tactics as well as long-range direction. "Here's the paradox: *there needs to be a plan, and the plan has to acknowledge that it will be departed from.*"[13]

So in addition to the content of the work of the organization, management needs to focus on the processes. The way we manage change is just as important for success as the substantive aspects of those changes. Management emphasis must be on helping the organization become better at diagnosing and solving problems. We need to legitimize self-examination, which has been denied in the past, and open up areas to change that have not previously been open or have been considered "untouchable."

In this new environment, managers will benefit from having a high tolerance for frustration, being willing to settle for little short-term successes in hope of obtaining greater long term payoffs, being open to influence and feedback from others, and being willing to take risks and experiment with alternative strategies in the face of more traditional norms and procedures.[14] As Robert Hass, head of Levi Strauss, put it, ". . . the controls have to be conceptual. It's the ideas of an organization that are controlling, not some manager with authority. Values provide a common language for aligning an organization's leadership and its people."[15]

TRAINING FOR BEHAVIORAL COMPETENCE

As well as involving and empowering every member of the staff to constantly question the status quo, organizational change is about training. Management should not only encourage staff to attend training, they must require it. In addition to requiring formal training, management must praise staff for pursuing a path of continuous learning through reading, attending external seminars, joining networking groups, and so on.

The central training department must institute a broad based organizational change activity with a focus on not only individuals but more importantly on systems. In consultation with line management, a long range educational program designed to increase effectiveness of the system can be prepared. Staff development and training will be for organizational and system renewal and effectiveness. Rather then as experts and teachers, the trainers will see themselves as consultants and change agents. The distinguishing characteristic of these change efforts will be a series of sessions for teams of staff in which "trainers" assist participants in combining training with problem solving.

In addition, moving from traditional skills training to an organization change effort may well mean that the organization has to deal with issues which are easy to ignore or avoid but which are crucial to the success of the effort. These issues have to do with the emphasis to be placed on development and the resources devoted to it, with implications regarding basic and sometimes uncomfortable issues such as influence, change in behavior and attitude, and with the role and competencies of the staff. Unless these issues are confronted the organization is likely to find that it is extremely difficult to sustain a meaningful change effort.[16]

Research library managers must see these issues, not solely as personnel activities, but rather as key priorities for themselves as managers. They must realize that one of the key factors determining whether or not we will succeed is the state of our organizations. A cohesive staff and organizational development program must become a priority.

A well-planned, formal training curriculum is absolutely essential to building an effective organizational culture. Training teaches staff to do things differently, which is where we should intervene in the cycle of behavioral change. Doing things differently leads to different results, and different results begin to change attitudes. These changed attitudes are necessary to modify the organizational culture. Training as part of an organizational change effort calls for new non-traditional approaches. Much of the content and method is based on the behavioral sciences rather than on traditional management theory or personnel techniques. Goals focus on developing behavioral competence in areas such as communication, decision making, team work, and problem solving, in addition to understanding and retention of principles and theories. The focus is on the total system of interdependent sub-organizational groupings (work units and teams) rather than upon individual staff as the object of training. Training as part of an organizational change effort utilizes experiential learning techniques rather than the traditional teacher centered subject matter programs.[17]

It does require considerable knowledge and skill, as well as a flexibility of response to be a successful manager of change. The organizational frontier facing the post industrial society that Schmidt[18] envisions is going to require all the skills multi-discipline managers can bring to bear on complex and unknown problems. The challenge to those of us who dare to help both ourselves and others to cope with this frontier is clearly expressed by Schmidt (1970) in a series of questions which outline the kinds of values, attitudes and beliefs needed:

- Am I prepared to live with uncertainty–to move before all the facts are in (they never are) or arranged in clear patterns (they seldom are)?
- Am I willing to risk failure from acting now on the basis of my best judgement rather than waiting for others to take the first chance?
- Can I stay open to new learning from every experience–my own and others?

Management development appears to be one of the preeminent challenges available to our profession. After all we are an organization-based profession and our managers have much of the leadership responsibilities for our profession. Unfortunately, with a few exceptions such as the ARL/OMS programs, the training and development of research library managers has been a haphazard process, largely ignoring the concepts of organizational change and development.

As library leaders struggle to address ever-complex environments and issues of response to rapid change, the opportunities of organizational development for stimulating innovation and creativity, will become seen as increasingly important. *To effectively manage in today's changing environment, an understanding of how change is designed and constructed in an organization, how small changes relate to strategic reorientations is required.*

There is a growing recognition of the important unique aspects of these concepts. Increasingly library managers are exploring the organizational development role as a significant complement to the more traditional part of their management repertoire. The main thing organizational development can do for our research libraries that nothing else can is help them design, implement, evaluate, and improve the substantive change processes they need to become the types of organizations they want to be. Organizational Development's contribution lies in developing processes to help with processes.[19]

BUILDING ORGANIZATIONAL UNITS

Even more important than the need to develop individual performance capabilities is the need for the research library manager to develop and manage collective performance. To see the organization as the unit of change is fundamental. The average manager's need for a new role identity as a builder of organizational units is probably the single most important purpose of any management development program. Yet most management development programs, failing to make the shift from managing individuals to managing teams, from managing organizational–rather than individual–efforts, continue to emphasize one-to-one management skills. The concept of the team approach is particularly relevant to the need to manage creatively the processes of adaptation and innovation and *being a team builder/manager is crucial to redefining management's role in these turbulent times.*

Team building in this context is the process of deliberately creating a team. It suggests something substantial that has to be constructed and that will go through several stages and take time to complete. Few teams develop to their full effectiveness without a good deal of conscious development. Effective teams have to be constructed methodically and painstakingly. Relationships have to be built, work methods clarified, and an energetic and positive climate created. An element of systematic planning and review must be brought to the task of developing teams.

The team manager builds openness and risk development, while trying to utilize energy and harness initiative. Being a team manager involves a distinctive management style; it requires a commitment to developing the resources of the group rather than to controlling it. A supervisor (which in Latin means gardener) must "tend" the team with considerable effort and care. Some managers build their people into an energetic, working team; others create groups that avoid facing issues and spend precious time passing the buck. But contrary to popular belief all groups are capable of development and the process of building better work teams can be learned.

CONCLUSION

As Peter Drucker emphasized, "The present is a time of great entrepreneurial ferment, where old and staid institutions suddenly have to become very limber." The research libraries that will succeed and flourish in the times ahead will be those "who have mastered the art of change: creating a climate encouraging the introduction of new procedures and new possibilities, encouraging anticipation of and response to external pressures, encouraging and listening to new ideas from inside the organization."[20]

To speak about change is well and good. Bringing about the kind of major system-oriented organizational changes necessary today is enormously complex. While effective intervention in complex systems is still largely an art, it can benefit from increased systematic thinking and the application of organizational development skills and strategies. Our efforts to reposition research libraries to serve information age universities in the twenty-first century can be facilitated by organizational development strategies. Current theory and practice of organizational development can help us as managers to relate process to content; recognize group and organizational-behavior issues, and understand the nature of resistance to change, where and how it is likely to occur, and how to deal with it.

Change for any individual or organization can be difficult, but it appears particularly difficult in large organizations and most particularly in large organizations that have been previously successful. These changes will not be easy, just necessary. In changing an organization's culture, it is essential to remember that many small steps create change. Singles win games, particularly when there are enough of them. If we focus on building small wins, making progress consistently, in the long run, they will add up to a win.

NOTES

1. Roeber, R.J.C., *The Organization in a Changing Environment*. (Reading, MA: Addison-Wesley, 1973):x.

2. Donald A. Schon, *Beyond the Stable State*. (New York: W.W. Norton and Company, Inc., 1971):17.

3. W.G. Bennis, *Organizational Development: Its Nature, Origins, and Prospects*. (Reading, MA: Addison-Wesley, 1969):2.

4. Philip G. Hanson and Bernard Lubin, "Organizational Development: Answers to Questions Frequently Asked by Managers," *Organizational Development Journal* 4,4 (1986): 40.

5. Schon, 64.

6. Ibid. 163.

7. Brownislaw Malinowski, *The Dynamics of Culture Change*. (New Haven: Yale University Press, 1945): 1.

8. Rosabeth Moss Kanter, *The Change Masters: Innovation and Entrepreneurship in the American Corporation*. (New York: Simon and Schuster, Inc., 1984): 305.

9. W. French, C. Bell, and R. Zawacki, "Mapping the Territory," in: *Organization Development: Theory, Practice and Research*, edited by W. French, C. Bell, and R. Zawacki, 5-12. Plano, TX: Business Publications, 1978.

10. B.T. Mayes and R. Allen, "Toward a Definition of Organizational Politics," *Academy of Management Review*, 2, (1977): 672-678.

11. K. Lewin, R. Lippitt, and R. White, "Patterns of Aggressive Behavior in Experimentally Created Social Climates," *Journal of Social Psychology* 10 (1939): 271-299.

12. K. Beene and M. Birnbaum, "Principles of Changing," in: *The Planning of Change*, edited by W.G. Bennis, K. Benne, and R. Chin, 331. New York: Holt, Rinehart and Winston, 1969.

13. Kanter, 359-60.

14. Philip G. Hanson and Bernard Lubin "Organization Development: Answers to Questions Frequently Asked by Managers," *Organizational Development Journal* 4,4 (1986): 43.

15. R. Howard, "Values Make the Company," *Harvard Business Review*, (Sept.-Oct. 1990):134.

16. Chris Argyris "Today's Problems with Tomorrow's Organizations," *The Journal of Management Studies*, 4,1, (1967): 31-55.

17. William B. Eddy, "From Training to Organization Change," *Personnel Administration*. (January-February, 1971):37-43.

18. W.H. Schmidt, *Organizational Frontiers and Human Values*. (Belmont, CA: Wadsworth Publishing Company, Inc., 1970): 4.

19. Peter B. Vail, "Seven Process Frontiers for Organization Development," in: *The Emerging Practice of Organization Development*, edited by Walter Sikes. Allan Drexler, and Jack Gant, 261-272. Virginia: NTL Institute for Applied Behavioral Science, 1989.

20. Kanter, 65.

The Maturing Worker in Technical Services

Kay Flowers

INTRODUCTION

Libraries in the Nineties will be affected by the same forces affecting other segments of society, and many decisions will be driven by these considerations. Two such forces could have a large effect on technical services in particular. The first of these is the rapid development and deployment of information processing technology. The second major trend is the aging of the workforce, affecting libraries as well as other industries. These two trends will not act in isolation. They will meet and interact in technical services to produce a stressful climate of change with the potential for great gains or serious problems in productivity. With the appropriate understanding of the situation, and appropriate management of change, most of the pitfalls can be avoided, and all of the advantages can be claimed.

THE AGING WORKFORCE

The "graying of America" has been discussed in the popular literature for some time. With increasing longevity (a lower death

---

Kay Flowers is Assistant University Librarian, Automated Services, Fondren Library, Rice University, Houston, TX.

[Haworth co-indexing entry note]: "The Maturing Worker in Technical Services." Flowers, Kay. Co-published simultaneously in the *Journal of Library Administration* (The Haworth Press, Inc.) Vol. 18, No. 3/4, 1993, pp. 145-158; and: *Catalysts for Change: Managing Libraries in the 1990s* (ed: Gisela M. von Dran and Jennifer Cargill) The Haworth Press, Inc., 1993, pp. 145-158. Multiple copies of this article/chapter may be purchased from The Haworth Document Delivery Center [1-800-3-HAWORTH; 9:00 a.m. - 5:00 p.m. (EST)].

© 1993 by The Haworth Press, Inc. All rights reserved.

rate), the portion of the population over sixty-five has gradually grown. In the decade of the nineties, however, society will experience the "maturing" of the workforce. By the year 2000, the average worker will be thirty-nine years old, and fifty-one percent of the workforce will be between the ages of thirty-five and fifty-four, while another eleven percent will be over fifty-five. The first wave of the "baby-boomers," those born between 1946 and 1961, will hit fifty-five the next year. At that age, they will be eligible to join AARP (the American Association of Retired Persons). Since the Age Discrimination in Employment Act of 1968 (ADEA) protects workers over the age of forty from discrimination based on age, any worker over 40 years of age is an "older" worker. By 2001, all baby-boomers will fit that definition.

Combined with this increase in the proportion of older workers will be a decline in the number of young people entering the labor force. Younger workers are often valued because they are more willing to fill entry level jobs and work for lower wages, particularly in some service areas such as the fast-food industry. Also, they are seen as providing "new blood" for other types of organizations. The baby-boomers did not have as many children as their parents; therefore, there are fewer children to enter the labor force due to this lower birth rate. As America approaches the year 2000, this shift from youth to maturity in the work force will become more and more apparent.

If economic trends as well as trends in longevity continue as they have in the past three decades, more people will want to work past retirement age. Though the eighties saw a large number of early retirements as industry retrenched, many of these workers still want jobs. Since fixed incomes are subject to inflationary pressure, many will seek to augment their savings through continuing to work. People not only experience greater longevity, they remain healthier longer. Since the ADEA has removed the mandatory retirement age in most job categories, there is nothing to restrict workers from working beyond the "normal" retirement age of sixty-five.

Implications of an Aging Workforce

Some have expressed concern about the impact the aging workforce will have on the workplace, but most of these concerns are based on stereotypes or incorrect information. In fact, these stereotypes are often the greatest hurdle facing the older worker. In general, the stereotype assumes the older worker has poor attendance, is more prone to accidents, is slower, has lower productivity, is less creative, is unwilling–or unable–to learn new skills, and resents younger management. The facts on aging and the older worker are much different.

First of all, the older worker is likely to have better attendance than the younger. In a review of the literature on factors affecting productivity, Smith (1990) reports that the older worker is more reliable and less likely to have either voluntary or involuntary absenteeism. The older worker also has a lower accident rate and a lower turnover rate than the younger worker. Therefore, rather than being a hindrance to the workplace, the older worker is an asset in dependability and safety.

While it is true that some faculties decline as part of the aging process, any slow down in the older worker depends more on the type of job rather than on age. For example, in jobs which are paced (such as assembly lines), older workers may have trouble keeping up with paces not consistent with their optimum rhythm (Garg 1991). In such a situation, older workers may have themselves moved to jobs where the pace is slower or where they are allowed to set their own pace. For less strenuous jobs, age is not a factor in productivity decline. Instead, when comparing job performance measures, there are often no differences in performance between older and younger workers, or the differences found are not correlated with age (Smith 1990). In his review of the research, Smith (1990) reports that various theories are advanced for why there are no age-related declines in productivity. One such factor would be moving to a less-demanding job, as mentioned earlier. Another idea is that an older worker may be in a position that did not require all of his/her available capacity, so the worker has reserve capacity available for stressful situations. Another theory suggests that when older workers maintain their skills, there is no productivity decline. Also, older workers are able to maintain their levels of productivity through compensations. The best example given in the literature is of typists. The older typists had a slower keystroke time than younger typists. However, their typing rate had not diminished because they had compensated for their slow-down by reading farther ahead in the document they were typing (Kimmel 1990). Finally, older workers benefit from the same factor that defines expertise: experience. Older workers are able to maintain their performance based on their ability to categorize problems and act quickly based on their long-term experience in a skill area (Smith 1990).

To say that an older worker is not creative is not accounting for all the facts. There are many people in their nineties making contributions to society. If older workers are perceived as uncreative, it may be because they are not asked to participate. In fact, several businesses have benefitted from the input of older workers (Kiechel 1990).

The training and retraining issue is probably the most damaging of all the older worker stereotypes. The older worker is seen as not open to training, so training is not offered (the perception is that the money is best spent investing in a younger worker). However,

> an age-related decline in rated job performance in 'knowledge' occupations ... is less likely to be associated with a loss of physical or mental skills and more likely to result from a deterioration in the quality of the information forming the knowledge base, from which new ideas are generated. (Davies and Sparrow 1985, 315)

Though training may have to be offered in different formats, it is critical to the creative input of the older worker.

Finally, many older workers *want* to work. Even those considering retirement would like to continue in a more flexible arrangement, either through part time work or job sharing schemes. Managers should not assume that all older workers are ready for the complete leisure of the traditional view of retirement.

While stereotypes should be avoided, there are, indeed, real declines in certain abilities with age. Most of these declines begin in a person's twenties and are gradual until after age sixty. The most dramatic declines, involving body strength such as would be needed in construction or work on the assembly line, are not relevant to the technical services area. Instead, declines in cognitive functioning, the abilities to solve problems, make decisions, and react quickly are more relevant. Though these faculties decline slowly across the life span, a person can adjust for these declines so that productivity is not affected.

Impacts in the Library

The older worker of the nineties will affect personnel issues in the library, but one finds more benefits in older workers than liabilities. First of all, the older worker will have more experience than others recently hired. This experience, in terms of on-the-job training, could save the library some of the money and time spent on training. In addition to experience, many mature workers demonstrate more stability. They have a lower tendency to change jobs and a greater incentive to stay in one place. Again, the savings accrued through lower turnover should not be dismissed. The flexibility desired by the older worker may work to the benefit of the library in scheduling flex time. Finally, the maturity as well as the wealth of history and experience with an institution that the older worker brings to the workplace is an advantage in most situations.

In spite of the evidence against stereotyping the older worker, there are legitimate concerns associated with the maturing labor force. The stability which makes the older worker a good investment may impede the ability of a library to attract and hire excellent candidates for job openings. The prevalence of two-income families makes it more difficult for a worker to move in middle-age, uprooting not only herself/himself but spouse and children as well. This same stability will make the older worker less likely to seek retraining or to change occupations. Finally, the unwillingness to move will make hiring decisions critical as turnover decreases. The older worker is specifically protected by the Age Discrimination in Employment Act of 1967 and additional legislation of 1978. Therefore, all personnel decisions must be carefully scrutinized for compliance.

THE CHANGING WORKPLACE

The workplace in which the older worker will find him or herself will not be static because a second trend affecting technical services is the increasing deployment of information processing technology. Therefore, the workplace of the nineties will be characterized by continuing technological advancement in many areas. As libraries have seen in the last two decades, there will be an increasing use of and dependence on technology for achieving production goals. As has been the case recently, there will be a continuing emphasis on productivity and quality with technology viewed as the means for achieving these two ends.

The application of technology to technical services processes is not new; however, the pace is picking up. The first systems, built in the sixties, lasted a decade, several developing into systems in use today. The early punch card technology of the late sixties gave way to the terminals of the seventies. The OCLC terminals bought by a library in 1979 were replaced in 1990, a life span of eleven years. However, this longevity is not likely to be repeated. The personal computer, as illustrated by the IBM PC, is just one example of the decreasing life expectancy of technology.

The first IBM personal computer was introduced in 1981 running on a 8086 chip, operating at 4 megahertz, with a monochrome monitor, 128K of memory and two floppy disks each holding 360 kilobytes of data. The systems selling for a comparable price today run on a 386 chip at 33 Megahertz. They come with color monitors using the virtual graphics adapter technology, 4 megabytes of memory, an 80 megabyte hard drive plus a floppy drive varying in capacity from 1.2 MB to 2.88 MB. The 486 machine is now the more advanced product, but the 586 chip is currently under development. In the workstation market, the development is even faster, and the prices are falling so that they are competitive with high-end personal computers.

There is no indication that this trend will slow down in the immediate future. The machine bought today will be obsolete in five years, no longer running the latest versions of the software needed. Most technical services departments are approaching or have reached the point where every employee needs a terminal or personal computer, thus increasing the impact of the shrinking equipment life spans. The complete replacement of all equipment in a technical services division every six to eight years is very expensive in hardware and training.

Mainframe systems are no different, though their cost prohibits their quick replacement. Nevertheless, software vendors, to remain competitive, will continue to develop software for the newer hardware products, thus driving the need for upgrades in the seven to ten year timeframe. In the nineties, all libraries will face equipment and system upgrades at least once, and perhaps more often.

In the library computing world, the mainframe and mini-computer are still well represented, but the move to smaller machines (downsizing) is becoming more prevalent. In downsizing, the workstation becomes more important, tied to the increasing importance of networks in the library environment. The existence of the Internet, and the development of the National Research and Education Network (NREN), have altered the library's view of both providing and obtaining information, making access over ownership more realistic. Cataloging information, now provided over dedicated lines, will move more to provision over networks. Other information products will be available over networks, and the first efforts at cataloging these resources have already begun.

How can this rate of change be illustrated? Consider one small academic library as an example of the changes that have occurred. This library had a locally developed circulation system and a locally developed acquisition system in 1978. That year, they changed to a batch ordering system for acquisitions and implemented an emergency manual circulation system when the in-house system failed. In 1979, they joined OCLC and bought a minicomputer-based circulation system. In 1980, a stand-alone word-processing system was purchased and the batch acquisition system was replaced by manual acquisitions records. The first personal computer, an M300, was bought for OCLC interlibrary loan access. In 1985, the first PC clone was purchased to transfer records from the old circulation system to diskette as part of the migration to a new integrated system. This system, installed in 1986, included circulation, cataloging, authority control, acquisitions, serials, and an online catalog, all activated in one year with new terminals required for all departments. In 1990, the OCLC terminals were replaced with M310s or equivalent workstations. In 1991, Passport and Prism were installed. That same year, the integrated system was upgraded to take advantage of the export function from OCLC, thus changing the manner in which records were loaded into the system. Finally, desktop publishing was established, using Macintoshes and Pagemaker. And during this span of years, the one PC has grown to 120, all running various software that requires training. Now all staff need to learn electronic mail. The average worker who photocopied cards for the card catalog in 1978 has been trained on OCLC (twice), an integrated system (twice), and a personal computer. The acquisition worker has been trained on an in-house system, a batch system, a manual system, and an integrated system, plus any personal computer training necessary, all in a span of fourteen years.

The library described is not unique and was able to benefit from the lessons learned by others. However, more than a hardware change was involved in each system change. With all these changes came the related problem of record conversion or the necessity of running dual systems. Training was needed each time a system changed or was upgraded. Procedures had to be revised, workflows had to be analyzed and changed, and all staff had to be incorporated in the process. Some tasks were no longer needed (e.g., the typists that typed subject headings on cards for the card catalog), so jobs had to be redesigned and staff reassigned. Additional equipment was almost always required, including training on the specific issues related to its maintenance and use. The rapid development of technology should be expected to continue, and the workplace will continue to incorporate a similar rate of change: change in equipment, change in workflow, change in procedures, and change in assignments.

INTERACTION OF THESE TWO TRENDS

When the rate of change described above is coupled with the more mature workforce, a stressful environment evolves. The pressures of change create new tasks for which older workers may feel unprepared. With uncertainty, limitations in adaptability may appear. If the workplace changes faster than training can be provided, the older worker may feel especially vulnerable. This build-up of concerns could lead to the resistance to change of which the older worker is accused. There are several areas, however, where this stress can be anticipated and preparations can be made. Three discussed here are ergonomic solutions, training, and change management.

An area of concern for older workers is the workplace itself. This area is under investigation by those studying human factors, the interaction of people and the equipment or products that are part of their lives, including those that occur in the workplace. This area has been described popularly as *The Psychology of Everyday Things* (Norman 1988). Known as ergonomists in other countries, human factors specialists have increased their research on the aging population in the last decade. In 1990, *Human Factors*, the journal of the Human Factors Society, dedicated an entire issue to aging (Czaja 1990). One area of study, for example, is the older driver and her abilities and limitations in operating vehicles. More relevant to this discussion, however, is a review of the older worker and the challenges facing her (Smith 1990). Other journals are also providing reviews of the interaction of aging and the workplace (Garg 1991). Human factors specialists are studying the effects of age on many tasks involving actions such as lifting, standing, and reaching, as well as cognitive tasks such as vigilance and decision-making.

The ergonomics of the workplace will assume a greater importance as the population ages. Workstations and jobs will have to be adjusted to meet the changing needs of the worker in order to assure continuing productivity. This need is easier to see in assembly lines where the strength of the worker is critical in job performance. As strength declines with age, workplace accommodations through job redesign or reassignment can maintain the productivity of the worker. In technical services departments, strength is not a performance criterion, but cognitive abilities are tied to job performance, and physical limitations are related to some injuries.

In general, the working environment should be brighter and quieter for the older worker (Garg 1991). The decline in vision associated with aging creates the need for more illumination to achieve the same visual acuity, even with the aid of visual correction. Also, the older worker might be more sensitive to noise. Since hearing also declines with age, noise can prove a greater distraction when trying to understand conversation and verbal instruction. These general environmental concerns should be kept in mind when assigning work space to older workers.

The computer workstation is the central source of ergonomic concern in technical services. With each change of equipment, the workstation will have to be re-evaluated for the comfort and productivity of the worker. For example, the work surface of the workstation, where the monitor and keyboard are placed, can be at standard desk height, but should be adjusted for the height of the person if that person is much taller or much shorter than average height. The keyboard should be positioned so that it is lower than the elbows. The monitor should be positioned so that the worker does not have to look up at it but rather focuses in a slightly downward manner. Since computers vary in their height, it may be necessary to place the system unit on the floor or next to the monitor rather than placing the monitor on top of the system unit in order to get the correct height (Dyer 1990).

Central to the workstation is the chair. Sitting in one place and performing data entry for extended periods of time can be very uncomfortable. There are reports of soreness in the back, neck, shoulders, and legs. Therefore, the appropriate chair for data entry, the most common task in technical services, is adjustable. The height should be adjustable, but several other dimensions should be as well. The seat should tilt forward. The seat back should be adjustable to be sure it supports the lumbar region of the back. The best chairs also have movable arms so that the forearm is supported while typing. One common complaint is discomfort in the thighs from pressure on the seat of the chair. Good, padded seats are the best kind. However, if padding alone does not relieve this pressure, a foot rest might be necessary. Posture is critical to comfort in the workplace (Dyer 1990).

Physical position in the workplace, and the way in which some tasks are performed, are related to repetitive strain injuries. Repetitive strain injuries (RSI) are the result of rapid and repetitive movements of parts of the body for long periods of time. In technical services and data entry, the movements associated with typing can produce RSI. Symptoms of this type of injury include numbness, swelling, or soreness in the affected area, usually the hands and fingers. There are many kinds of repetitive strain injuries, but the type that has received the most attention recently is carpal tunnel syndrome. Carpal tunnel syndrome is often the result of a lack of support for the wrist causing flexing during pauses in typing, or typing from an incorrect position (with the wrists bent up constantly). The older worker, with a gradual reduction in joint flexibility, combined with a rising risk of arthritis, may be particularly vulnerable to carpal tunnel syndrome. Therefore, the ergonomic workstation is particularly important for the continuing health of the older worker.

Another characteristic of the aging worker is the gradual deterioration of vision. One sign of this decline is the need to use bifocal lenses to see near and distant objects (a loss of accommodation and a shift to farsightedness). Bifocal lenses correct the problem for most daily activities by providing two corrections: one for viewing items close to oneself, and one for viewing items farther away. However, they provide additional difficulties when used with terminals which are often placed between these two distances. Since library work often involves comparing information on the screen with information in a book or on paper, workers must alternate between looking at the book and looking at the screen. Bifocals complicate this process. Those requiring bifocals are often seen straining their neck back in order to look out the bottom of their lenses. This posture exacerbates neck and back strain resulting from general use of the terminal. The best solution suggested at this time is a separate pair of glasses for terminal use coupled with a stand attached to the terminal for material to be entered, thus using one focal distance for data entry and data to be entered.

Training

The correct furniture will not guarantee the high productivity levels desired in technical services departments. The rapid rate of system and equipment change will create a large need for training and retraining as well as workplace redesign. Each software enhancement will also require training. Thus, technical services workers will need to be continually upgrading their skills in order to be productive.

As discussed earlier, the older, more stable workforce is perceived as not fond of training or change. The lack of young people to hire, however, means that it is the older worker who will need training. Rapid technological innovations have made the obsolescence of knowledge and skills a real issue.

> Employers and professional organizations are starting to accept their responsibilities in providing opportunities for learning, hoping to motivate their staffs to update their work skills . . . the motivation to learn and the realization that one's skills are outdated must be personal. (Cargill and Webb, 1988, p. xii)

It is the realization and motivation that are likely to be difficult with the older worker. As pointed out earlier, the older worker can be trained as well as the younger worker; however, different methods will be needed.

In training the older worker, the lecture methods which work for younger employees are not as effective for the worker who has been out of school for over thirty years. Oral instruction is affected by declines in short-term memory, a decline that is part of the normal aging process. Instead, employers should use self-paced instruction and methods that leave the learner in control of the process while reinforcing learning objects and providing regular feedback (Wilcox 1990). Kiechel (1990) suggests that a trainer should help a worker "unlearn the old drill, proceed at her own pace . . . provide lots of examples as well as experts . . . then get out of her way" (p. 184). One company found that such changes actually shortened the training period of older workers in comparison to younger workers (Wilcox 1990).

Change Management

Many of these concerns for the older worker are equally applicable for all workers and could be addressed through effective change management. The older worker's perceived resistance to change underscores this need. Change management covers a set of techniques designed to encourage all workers to accept a change and assist in its implementation. At its heart, change management requires extensive communication about the nature and extent of the change involved. Most employees fear change because they fear for their jobs. The sooner such fears are shown to be groundless, the sooner true acceptance of the change can begin. If the fears are not groundless, and some workers will be laid off, early explanation of options may help alleviate tension and fear.

Many authors also suggest involving as many people as possible in the activity producing change.

> The worker himself, from the beginning, needs to be integrated as a resource into the planning process. From the beginning he has to share supervisors' thinking through work and process, tools and information. His knowledge, his experience, his needs are resources to the planning process. The worker needs to be a partner in it. (Drucker 1975, 34)

If people participate in planning a project, there is a greater possibility that they will "buy in" to the process and work for the successful implementation of the new system or procedures. Where possible, discussions should be delegated to the people involved. If ergonomic furniture is necessary, allow a committee to evaluate the proposed furniture and layout. Ask groups of workers to assist in training. Giving workers as much control as possible will keep them involved in the change and increase their flexibility.

Finally, the concerns regarding the response of older workers to younger supervisors would be alleviated through the same techniques employed in change management: "a request for his advice on tough decisions, an occasional bow to his expertise, a pat on the back, as public as possible" (Kiechel 1990, 186). Of course, this recommendation embodies good management practice for any worker at any age, and it should not be forgotten during a hectic period of change.

Budget Impact

The processes and changes described above, dealing with the maturing workforce in a rapidly changing technological environment, are not cheap. Money will be needed for the new technology, for both the equipment and initial training. Managers may find it hard to justify and find money for ergonomic redesign of the workplace and retraining of workers. However, with current emphases on productivity and quality, coupled with emerging laws covering workstations, money should be found. The ultimate payback for the library will be the increased productivity of a fully-trained, involved, productive workforce.

This article has discussed some of the impacts of the maturing American workforce on library technical services departments. The increasing dependence on technology plus its rapid development will create tensions and problems in technical services that will require creative solutions. However, if stereotypes are ignored, and proper training, ergonomic design, and change management are employed, the result could be the most productive decade of this century, setting the stage for more gains in the next.

REFERENCES

Cargill, Jennifer, and Webb, Gisela. *Managing Libraries in Transition.* Phoenix: Oryx Press, 1988.

Czaja. S. J. (Ed.) 1990. Aging [Special Issue]. *Human Factors.* 32(5).

Davies, D. R. and P. R. Sparrow. (1985). "Age and Work Behavior." In Neil Charness (Ed.) *Aging and Human Performance.* New York: John Wiley & Sons.

Drucker, Peter. *Management: Tasks, Responsibilities, Practices.* New York: Harper & Row, 1975.

Garg, Arun. (1991). "Ergonomics and the Older Worker." *Experimental Aging Research.* 17:143-155.

Johnston, W. B. and A. E. Packer. (1987). *Workforce 2000: Work and Workers for the Twenty-first Century.* Indianapolis, IN: Hudson Institute, 1987.

Kiechel, W. (1990). "How to Manage Older Workers." *Fortune.* 122(12):183-186 (November 5, 1990).

Kimmel, D. C. (1990) *Adulthood and Aging.* New York: John Wiley & Sons.

Norman, Donald. *The Psychology of Everyday Things.* New York: Basic Books, 1988.

Wilcox, J. (1990). "Getting Older, Getting Better." *Training and Development Journal.* 44(8): 9-10.

The Role of the Collection Development Librarian in the 90s and Beyond

Maria Otero-Boisvert

Collection development librarians both as administrators and as selectors are currently facing tremendous changes in the way they do their work. Information is now coming in a great variety of formats. Technology is a swiftly moving stream which they must be able to navigate successfully. In times of budgetary constraints, bibliographers must have the political wherewithal to present and defend their agenda in the larger university community. The professional literature is replete with discussions of future scenarios and the library's place in them. The two issues which keep recurring in these discussions are: (1) the budgetary constraints which almost all institutions are now enduring; and (2) the impact of electronic technology on academic research. This article will explore the changing role of the collection development librarian in the present day context and attempt to define the characteristics, skills and knowledge which will be required on the job. Finally, the article will discuss different approaches to acquiring these skills.

LITERATURE SURVEY

One doesn't have to dig too deeply to unearth the proliferation of articles discussing the future of libraries. Indeed, our proximity to

---

Maria Otero-Boisvert is Head of the Mallinckrodt Library, Loyola University, Chicago, IL.

[Haworth co-indexing entry note]: "The Role of the Collection Development Librarian in the 90s and Beyond." Otero-Boisvert, Maria. Co-published simultaneously in the *Journal of Library Administration* (The Haworth Press, Inc.) Vol. 18, No. 3/4, 1993, pp. 159-170; and: *Catalysts for Change: Managing Libraries in the 1990s* (ed: Gisela M. von Dran and Jennifer Cargill) The Haworth Press, Inc., 1993, pp. 159-170. Multiple copies of this article/chapter may be purchased from The Haworth Document Delivery Center [1-800-3-HAWORTH; 9:00 a.m. - 5:00 p.m. (EST)].

© 1993 by The Haworth Press, Inc. All rights reserved.

the end of the century and the coming of the new millennium has given birth to innumerable publications in every imaginable field, all of which share the same concern, "What will become of us?" Librarians are no exception. Peter Lyman tackles the issues in "The Library of the (Not-So-Distant) Future" in the journal *Change* (1991). He focuses on topics such as the changing nature of scholarly communication, the increasing volume of scholarly communication and the rising cost of library labor and infrastructure. Both Erwin Welsch in "Back to the Future: A Personal Statement on Collection Development in an Information Culture" (1989) and Immler and Mouw in "Collections Development and Acquisitions" (1989) describe in some detail the wonders of the future bibliographer's or selector's workstation. Without ever leaving their seat, selectors will be able to use their personal computers to carry out every aspect of their work. The process these authors describe have a faculty person turning to their pc at home to check the library catalog for a new title. Not finding it there, they access a library form electronically and transmit their purchase request via e-mail to the library system which routes it automatically to the appropriate bibliographer. This electronic process continues on through the presearch, order, processing, cataloging and patron-notification stages. Both articles emphasize the fact that the technology to make this scenario possible already exists in various components. All that is needed, they claim, are a few programs written to make different systems compatible. One finds these scenarios both exciting and troubling at the same time. Yes, this is the direction we want to go in, and yes, we even recognize the fact that many of the first steps have already been taken. But isn't it optimistic to expect the faculty to leap with unanimous joy at the prospect of the virtual library? How many of us know and even respect faculty members who refuse to work with the online catalog and still type their manuscripts page by painful page?

The concept of the virtual book is explored at length in Kurzweil's three part series on "The Future of Libraries" published in *Library Journal* (1992). Once again, we are invited to explore our current paradigms and rethink the concepts of "Library," "Book" and "Information" which we have long taken for granted. It is all rather heady stuff. In his provocative article, "Needed: User-Responsive Research Libraries," Richard Dougherty tells us what he thinks it will take to foster a "technology rich, user-responsive campus information environment" (Dougherty 1991, 62). He speaks of the two "myths" which have been accepted as fact by library professionals for decades: that bigger libraries are better libraries and that scholars know how to competently use the library for research. Dougherty believes that electronic libraries in their current form make a sham of the first myth, even though it is still widely held. The second myth he takes on is a little more threatening for librarians. Surveys have shown, Dougherty states, that faculty believe the library to be a minor source of information, a supplementary as opposed to a primary source. Worse yet, these same studies show that faculty don't really trust librarians and, in fact, question their competence (Dougherty 1991, 60). It would seem that there is work to be done in the area of public relations on campus.

Aside from the printed literature there is also a wide array of discussions taking place on electronic list services. One of them, COLLDV-L, is a relatively new discussion list moderated by Lynn F. Sipe of the University of Southern California. Although subscribers were quick to plug in to the service, the discussion was slow to warm up. In early October of 1992, the moderator posted a lengthy text prepared by several librarians, members of the Policy and Planning Committee of the Collection Management and Development Section of ALCTS. The members of this committee kindled the electronic discussion by presenting a series of thirteen "Issues and Trends" which they had identified as being important for the immediate to mid-term future. After outlining the issues, they appended a short abstract to each. At the top of their list was the issue of "Budget Allocation and Accountability." The point they made is that collection development officers, now more than ever, must have the skills and information necessary to defend their budgets. "Collection development librarians face challenges posed by dwindling resources and ever-expanding ways to allocate them. To meet these challenges successfully, we must find ways to provide both access and appropriate ownership. We need to develop models which acknowledge the continuing importance of traditional (albeit) reduced collecting yet allow for inclusion of new technologies..." (Parts 1-2, posted Oct. 12, 1992). In the midst of a national recession, and at a time when most college and research libraries are being forced to discontinue subscriptions, cut back on book budgets, freeze positions, and reduce staffing levels, collection development librarians are forced to present ever more sophisticated budget justifications and cost analyses.

The "Issues and Trends" discussion on COLLDV-L which reached the crux of the matter is found in Part Three: "Recruitment, Education and Management of Human Resources in a Changing Environment" (Parts 3-5, posted October 12, 1992). The writers felt that the basic duties and responsibilities of collection development librarians, whether part-time selectors or administrators, have changed considerably. Today's collection development librarian, they imply, must be financially savvy, politically aware and electronically literate. How many of us can claim to be all three? What training did we receive in library school to prepare us for our present reality? Very little in the majority of cases. "No matter how well educated or trained, collection management librarians can feel unprepared to cope with their current working environment. The ability to manage and adapt to change is becoming far more important than 'knowledge of the book trade' as a prerequisite for success" (Parts 3-5, posted October 12, 1992). Flexibility, an openness to new format, new ways of thinking, new responsibilities, what a challenge lays ahead for us!

BUDGETING IN DIFFICULT TIMES

Meredith Butler and Hiram Davis published an article on the need for strategic planning in the 90s in *College & Research Libraries* (September 1992). In it they set the stage for their discussion by describing the current environment most of us are working in: "For those of us leading academic libraries in the 1990s, the forces pressing us back include budgetary reductions, rapidly rising costs, reduced staffing, increasing complexity, escalating demands, and a national temper that has lost patience with higher education–some might say, a national temper that has lost faith in the value of higher education" (Butler and Davis, 393). One might argue that the idea of having to justify collections budgets is by no means a new one. Bibliographers have been doing it for a long time. The complicating factor is that we seem to be fighting for the same small slice of an ever shrinking pie. Simply put, there is more at stake these days.

Frank Immler and James R. Mouw explain just why collection development funds are particularly susceptible in difficult times: "Any library's book budget becomes vulnerable during a time of severe and sudden retrenchment. The Collections budget is not connected to people, so no one loses a job; it is not related to anything immediately affecting the user, so no one notices that books are not being acquired. The collections budget usually is a sizable amount of money, readily identified and easy to grab" (Immler and Mouw 1989, 119). What *is* totally new is the complexity of the information available and the ways it must be manipulated. The ALCTS committee describe it this way in their electronic document: "The spread of automated systems among libraries and library vendors and the development of subject based cost-indexes offer some of the elements needed for budget modeling. Comparative data by library size and type, broken down by commonly defined subject and format criteria, is a compelling need . . ." (Parts 1-2, posted October 12, 1992).

The typical bibliographer today will need to have some basic accounting skills, budgeting skills, knowledge of spreadsheet applications, negotiations skills with which to approach vendors and utilities, basic salesmanship, grant writing and administration, up-to-date knowledge of currency fluctuations around the world and world market forces, to name just a few. Clearly an M.A. in French literature coupled with today's M.L.S. does not prepare a bibliographer to do the kind of financial analysis and budget management that the current economic environment requires. It is quickly becoming apparent that today's collection manager would benefit from the coursework in an M.B.A. program. Additionally, one or two courses in Higher Education Administration would be equally useful (i.e., What is the difference between a provost and a chancellor? What is the role of the faculty senate? What is the purpose of the tenure process? How does a university allocate funds and what is the political process involved?). While it is true that most library students have the option of venturing into the Business School and the School of Education at their universities on their own and registering for these courses, how many of them know enough to do so?

How many of them were able to anticipate the need without the appropriate guidance?

THE NEW TECHNOLOGY

Issue number 6 as proposed by the ALCTS committee in their COLLDV-L discussion, centered on the integration of electronic formats into the existing culture of collection development librarians. "[We] must know how to select computer files that may be full-text, bibliographic, numeric, or even multi-media. In so doing, we must consider how to acquire, provide access, and then service these new resources [. . .] Organizationally, libraries and librarians must become more sophisticated about the new culture of information technology . . ." (Part 6, posted Oct. 12, 1992). Earlier in this article, we spoke of the bibliographer's workstation which was connected to the library's system, the wider university network, national and international networks, as well as numerous commercial databases. The problem underlined is that, while we may be nominally prepared to meet this future scenario, the majority of university faculty today are not. Peter Lyman talks about the "library as network": "Thus, the network is a valid image of the library as understood as a medium for the acquisition, storage and circulation of texts, particularly if it leads to the creation of shared resources. The network may become a medium for making information public. The patron of the online library will browse through digital texts and images, select and download research materials, and print them, possibly for a fee" (Lyman, 1991, 40). The author himself is quick to point out that this scenario will rely on the library patrons' willingness to change their "habits of information literacy." What role might the collection development librarian play in bringing about this change? In their liaison role to the various academic departments, colleges and institutes, they have an opportunity to interact with the faculty and students in ways which will further the information agenda. There is a strong political role to be played out here as well. If the academic departments need more pcs with mainframe access and telecommunications capabilities, the library can assist them write grant proposals for capital funding. If bibliographers serve on Faculty Senates or other similar bodies within their institutions, they can make the case for networking on campus in those forums. If Academic Computing doesn't know how to approach the academic departments or the university administration on the issue of information literacy, librarians certainly have years of experience in that area which may be of use. All of these activities can be seen as outgrowths or extensions of the bibliographers' traditional liaison roles.

In an article entitled, "Opening a Universitywide Dialogue About Electronic Information Resources," Carol Hughes cautions us that "Local faculty and university administrators may have quite different visions of the future information needs of the campus and different views of the impact which electronic information will have on the way they will perform research and teaching within their disciplines [. . .] There may be no vision at all, if academic colleagues have not been discussing these issues among themselves" (Hughes 1991, 85). This vacuum, if you will, may be seen as an opportunity for bibliographers to step in and build coalitions for the future. Recent history has shown that the libraries and the academic computing centers have been the two focal points of electronic advances within the university setting. To date, though, these two units have not cooperated to the extent that they should to create a university-wide information infrastructure. "The implementation of a strategy for the complete integration of information technology and electronic resources into traditional academic structures, such as the library, the computer center, and other campus units, could deeply affect the work lives of a wide range of faculty, students and staff" (Hughes 1991, 85). Obviously, the success of any project of this magnitude depends on the power of the vision it is built on and the extent to which we are able to *sell it*. The faculty and administration have to *buy in* or the project will fail. The bibliographer's role thus becomes that of sales representative or even political lobbyist.

Beverly Watkins has written an article on this very topic, "Widespread Collaboration With Computer Centers is Seen as Essential to the Library of the Future" in the *Chronicle of Higher Education* (February 26, 1992, A30). Her article is a brief discussion of the report written by Richard Dougherty and Carol Hughes for the Research Libraries Group. Entitled "Preferred Futures for Libraries," the report is is a result of a series of workshops for library directors and university administrators from over 41 universities. The main focus of the Watkins article is that to successfully implement the ideal of the virtual library through the widespread use of "universal workstations" hooked up to electronic networks, the library must work very closely with the computing center and the faculty. "Faculty attitudes will have a major impact on determining the nature and scope of future information environments in higher education" (Watkins 1992, A30).

Once again, we find that the key to success in the electronic future is the skillful application of traits such as salesmanship, interpersonal relations, political savvy and technical expertise. The challenge is a major one for most collection development librarians (the author of this article included). Where they may have once taken refuge in their scholarly selection activities with only occasional forays into the academic departments they serve (upon invitation, of course), they must now become players in the academic arena. Can sales reps, politicians and financial analysts be made out of scholarly bibliofiles? Do we need every selector to be a technocrat? To some degree the answer is yes, we must. What is more, we must do so without turning our backs on the traditional responsibilities, formats and resources. The authors of the COLLDV-L discussion end Part Six of their "Issues and Trends" document by stating that: "We should actively promote the continuing value of the traditional print collections, collections that will continue for some time to be at the center of our collection management development mission" (Part 6, posted October 13, 1992). In this the ALCTS authors are in complete agreement with most of the opinions being expressed today in the literature. Even that guru of technology, Raymond Kurzweil, in prophesying the advent of the virtual book admits that the printed version will enjoy a long and lingering farewell. In the middle of the electronic explosion, we will continue to buy books. In the depths of a national recession, we will continue to serve as cultural guides through the information maze.

HOW DO WE GET THERE FROM HERE?

Richard Dougherty's article in Library Journal (1991) ends with an exhortation to library professionals to learn from prior mistakes and build on their strengths. Although he is speaking about library professionals in general, Dougherty's comments may be applied to collection development librarians in particular, "There is general agreement that more professionals are needed who possess well-developed interpersonal skills, greater knowledge of information policy issues, and greater political skills. We need people with greater knowledge of traditional management skills such as finance and strategic planning, and individuals who possess entrepreneurial talent" (Dougherty 1991, 61). The interesting thing about this laundry list of desired traits is that they are all teachable. There is no need for an individual to self-select themselves out of a career in collection management because they are lacking in one or two areas. The question becomes, at what point do we acquire these skills?

There are three opportunities for building a collection development cadre that is prepared to meet the future as described above. First, there is the earliest possible phase, recruitment. Second, there is the middle phase of library school education and lastly, there is the ongoing, final phase of continuing education. Recruitment can be seen either as recruitment into the profession at the point of the masters program or at the point at which the fresh new degree holder is on the job market. Whatever group takes on the responsibility for recruitment could organize any number of efforts. Some examples might be formal mentoring programs in the second year of study, visits by professionals to library school classrooms, guest lecturer appointments for collection development administrators, etc. Admittedly, these are not innovative concepts, these techniques have been applied successfully in the past with various groups. The only novelty lies in their application to this particular variety of librarians-to-be.

The quality, structure and content of the M.L.S. degree program is a much discussed topic. The current electronic dialog being held on listserves such as COLLDV-L bears witness to the fact that it still holds our interest as a profession. Of all the "Trends and Issues" put forward by the ALCTS committee, the one which has generated the most response is the issue of professional education. Interestingly, some of the more active participants have been library school educators who have been monitoring the discussion very closely, adding their input judiciously and soliciting further opinions. The Association of College and Research Libraries has very recently published a statement crafted by their Professional Education Committee. The statement attempts to describe "the nature of academic librarianship" and the education needed to prepare for it (ACRL 1992, 590). This document makes it very clear that the educational mission of the professional program lies in providing only the baseboard from which to spring. "In laying the foundation of a librarian's career, professional programs are responsible for teaching techniques for analyzing information needs in particular environments; teaching principles related to the collection, preservation, retrieval, and use of information; and developing an individual's understanding of the nature and use of information technologies" (ACRL 1992, 591).

The statement sends a very strong message that any specific skills beyond the theory outlined above should be picked up through continuing education. It identifies three sources of continuing education: the employer, the professional associations and other graduate degree programs. One can identify several problems with this approach. The first which comes to mind is the fact that employers do not always offer continuing education opportunities to all employees in a fair and equal manner. Continuing education costs money and often involves travel expenses and professional leave time. Usually, the perceived "stars" of an organization are singled out for favors of this sort while the rank and file librarians are left to their own devices. Many institutions can not even afford to send their stars to workshops and conferences. The net result is that not every professional has the same access to continuing education.

The second objection which can be made is that this document is sending out the message that an M.L.S. is only a partial preparation. The ambitious librarian who wants to build a solid career must pay, not only for the M.L.S. but also for at least one other graduate degree. Why not just go to law school or business school? It may well be cheaper, quicker and more remunerative. Haven't students the right to expect a professional degree which adequately prepares them for entree to the market place without the need for additional expenditure of time and money? Another troubling aspect of the ACRL statement is that it persists in defining librarianship as primarily a scholarly endeavor. Perhaps this is yet another myth which needs to be exploded. The real life, day-to-day activities of a library administrator and most collection development librarians have more in common with the business world than the scholarly one. Selectors have long been seen as the last bastion of scholarly activity within the library field. But as this article has shown, even they must enhance their knowledge of academic fields with a great deal of practical management, administrative, political and technical expertise. Perhaps it is time that the profession recognize this fact.

REFERENCES

Association of College and Research Libraries. Professional Education Committee. "Education for Professional Academic Librarianship." *College & Research Libraries News* 53, no. 9 (October 1992): 590-591.

Butler, Meredith and Hiram Davis. "Strategic Planning as a Catalyst for Change in the 1990s." *College & Research Libraries* 53, no. 8 (September 1992): 393-403.

Dole, Wanda. "Acquisitions and Collection Development: 2001–The End User." *Library Acquisitions: Practice & Theory* 12 (1988): 249-253.

Dougherty, Richard M. "Needed: User-Responsive Research Libraries." *Library Journal* 116, no. 1 (January 1991): 59-62.

Gonzalez-Kirby, Diana. "Case Studies in Collection Development: Setting an Agenda for Future Research." *Collection Building* 11, no. 2 (1991): 2-9.

Hughes, Carol. "Opening a Universitywide Dialogue About Electronic Information Resources." *College & Research Libraries News* 52, no. 2 (February 1991): 84-87.

Immler, Frank and Mouw, James R. "Collections Development and Acquisitions." In *The Academic Library in Transition: Planning for the 1990s*, edited by Beverly Lynch, 118-158. New York: Neal-Schuman, 1989.

"Issues and Trends for Collection Management." A Listservice discussion introduced by the members of the Policy and Planning Committee of the Collection Management and Development Section of ALCTS. Beginning on October 7, 1992. *COLLDV-L* (Library Collection Development List) is moderated by Lynn F. Sipe, AUL for Collection Development, Univ. of Southern California.

Johnson, Peggy. "The Future has Arrived Prematurely: MRDF and Collection Development." *Technicalities* 9, no. 9 (September 1989): 10-13.

Kurzweil, Raymond. "The Future of Libraries Part 1: The Technology of the Book." *Library Journal* 117, no. 1 (January 1992): 80-82.

_____. "The Future of Libraries Part 2: The End of Books." *Library Journal* 117, no. 3 (February 15, 1992): 140-141.

_____. "The Future of Libraries Part 3: The Virtual Library." *Library Journal* 117, no. 5 (March 15, 1992): 63-64.

Lyman, Peter. "The Library of the (Not-So-Distant) Future." *Change* (January/February 1991): 34-41.

Rutstein, Joel S. "Collection Development Confronts the 90s: Emerging New Challenges." A Special Issue of *Colorado Libraries* 16 (March 1990): 5-22.

Smith, Eldred. "The Print Prison." *Library Journal* 117, no. 2 (February 1, 1992): 48-51.

Watkins, Beverly T. "Widespread Collaboration With Computer Centers Is Seen as Essential to the Library of the Future." *Chronicle of Higher Education* (February 26, 1992): A30.

Welsch, Erwin K. "Back to the Future: A Personal Statement on Collection Development in an Information Culture." *Library Resources and Technical Services* 33 (January 1989): 29-36.

The Budget as a Planning Tool

William K. Black

INTRODUCTION

Libraries have been rocked by change. It has been a difficult transition from the stability and growth of the late sixties to the complexities of the nineties. We now deal with complex fiscal, technological, and accountability issues that have centrally affected the role of the library as a service unit. Dealing with change is the normal order of the day for library administrators. The role of the library continues to evolve within a shifting environment that demands effective leadership and management. These forces have moved libraries forward from information, print-driven repositories dependent upon local collections, to critical units in a larger information environment, informing and educating users regardless of information format or location. As we attempt to deal with the challenges of the 1990s and beyond, we need to recognize that the budget process is an integral component of our planning cycle, placing critical value upon the plans and priorities that are developed.

FORCES PROMOTING CHANGE

The nature of today's libraries has been affected dramatically by what Bertha Almagro refers to as the "unholy alliance formed by

---

William K. Black is Associate Professor, Library Development and Project Management, Iowa State University, Ames, IA.

[Haworth co-indexing entry note]: "The Budget as a Planning Tool." Black, William K. Co-published simultaneously in the *Journal of Library Administration* (The Haworth Press, Inc.) Vol. 18, No. 3/4, 1993, pp. 171-188; and: *Catalysts for Change: Managing Libraries in the 1990s* (ed: Gisela M. von Dran and Jennifer Cargill) The Haworth Press, Inc., 1993, pp. 171-188. Multiple copies of this article/chapter may be purchased from The Haworth Document Delivery Center [1-800-3-HAWORTH; 9:00 a.m. - 5:00 p.m. (EST)].

inflation, rising prices, and devaluation."[1] Just as powerfully, this role has been transformed by other forces as well, such as the growing information needs of a knowledge-based clientele, use of technology for managing larger and larger quantities of information, budget cutbacks, a greater call for accountability within our institutions, governing boards, and governments, and an increase in the diversity of our users. Within higher education we are confronted by increasing demands for accountability in the use of resources due to a decade of strong inflation for materials, particularly from abroad, and high tuition increases, coupled with shrinking resources from national and state deficits.

A key factor which has affected the nature of the library's role has been the rapid pace of technological change. Libraries have seen an explosion of information in various formats which has presented numerous challenges for its acquisition, access, storage and legal use. Along with cost increases, budget cutbacks, increasing calls for accountability, and the changing face of the user, new technology has been a forceful player in the reforging of the library mission. The advance of computer applications and networks in bibliographic access mechanisms and library support functions has increased complexities and opened alternatives that did not previously exist. It has presented many challenges to the decisions of bibliographic control, access and use.

The pace of technological change has also presented an opportunity to improve how we account for information and how the researcher finds it, to consider viable alternatives for accessing and delivering materials that we need not own, and to change our methods of managing libraries. "In summary, the result of this rapidity of technological change is to force great emphasis upon planning, for at the same time that the rate of change of technology makes planning more different, it also makes it more important. The wealth of technology provides a choice of options that simply was not available before. This choice in turn forces a focus upon what is to be accomplished and why, and this in turn leads inevitably toward a programmatic emphasis in planning and budgeting."[2]

As we move into the 21st century, we know we must continue to follow careful management strategies in order to serve as appropriate trustees of the resources and services we provide to a changing clientele. Libraries will continue to face a growing need for information and its interpretation as they are, at the same time, presented with complex choices in the access and delivery of multiple forms of that information. We will be subject to continuing review of the effectiveness of our organizations. Libraries will grow increasingly dependent upon one another as they attempt to meet the research needs of their users within limited budgets. As Carla Stoffle has pointed out, "Today we are setting the philosophical and policy foundation for library and information services for the 21st century and beyond; shaping the information agenda in our institutions and in the national arena; structuring access tools and creating new information products; and establishing the research agenda and research patterns which will enable us to keep information services and structures relevant to users' changing needs. The capability exists, or soon will, to control, organize, structure and disseminate information in ways we could scarcely imagine in the past. We will be limited only by our own lack of vision and unwillingness to change."[3]

PLANNING AND CHANGE

As the library field has been faced with rapid technological change and decreased purchasing power, many libraries have seen the need to place their decision-making process within a more formal structure. Many institutions have adopted strategic planning as a means of organizing and prioritizing library operations (see Figure 1). "Active engagement in the institution's planning and policy-setting processes has particular importance for today's . . . libraries. Strategic planning provides library directors and their staffs with an excellent process for addressing policy vacuums and for overcoming some political limitations and organizational barriers. It is a process that shifts the library, both organizationally and functionally, from a reactive mode of coping with the present to a proactive mode of envisioning and moving toward a clearly defined and desired future. . . . Strategic planning assists the library in being responsive to constituent and organizational needs in order to develop strategies sufficiently flexible to take advantage of today's unprecedented confusion of opportunities."[4]

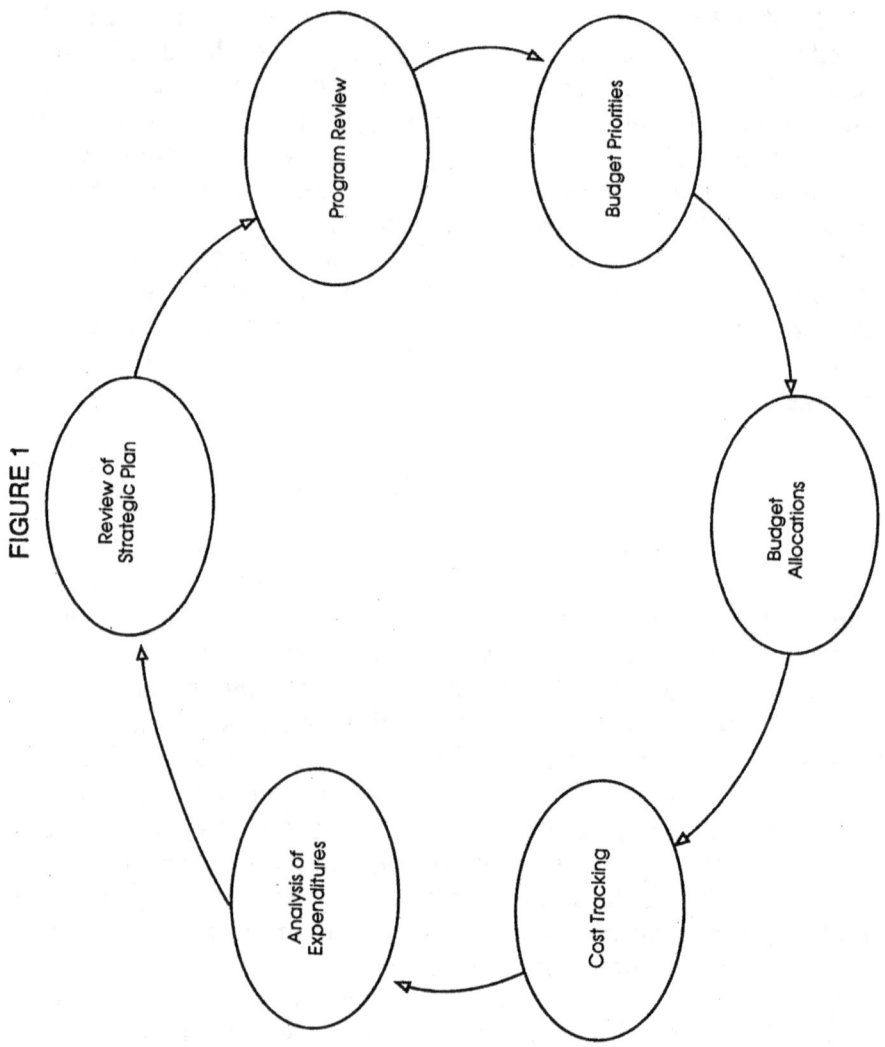

FIGURE 1

The process of strategic planning involves full participation within the library organization and with external constituencies to review the strengths and weaknesses of the organization and the environment it serves. This comprehensive review should result in the establishment of realistic goals and measurable objectives within the context of the library's capabilities and the users' needs. The outcomes include an assessment of the user base, review of programs and services, and a plan of action that pulls together human and financial resources and program activities into a realistic program for success. The effective planning review process should be a responsive, communicative and team-building endeavor that results in a clear and attainable organizational plan designed for a defined audience. It should be a continuous process that helps the library deal with a shifting environment composed of changing user needs, new information technologies, and inconstant revenue bases.[5]

BUDGETARY MANAGEMENT

Budget as a Planning Tool

Budgeting is really a method for placing the library plan into a financial framework. It defines objectives, identifies resources and assigns them to the priorities of the library in order to obtain the stated objectives. And it provides a financial means of assessing accomplishment of the library's goals and objectives. As libraries utilize a planning process to effectively create a strategy for managing in these times of challenge, it is important to recognize the budget as a critical element in the development and execution of the plan of operation, not simply as a financial accounting system, but rather as an integral component of creative library management. "In my opinion, the two essential components in library management for the future will be budgeting–the justifying, allocating, raising, and managing of library funds, and creativity–the ability to create a new product, service, program, process, procedure or innovative solution to a problem."[6] If we are to adopt an effective planning process in which to sort the management decisions and overall priorities, we must also develop a responsive budgeting process that flows from the plan and relates dynamically to the programs of the library. "Scarce resources and economic recessions have made resource allocation decisions more critical and difficult in both the profit and not-for-profit sectors. With fewer funds available, the decision as to how to use those resources becomes more important. Budgeting is a managerial tool which facilitates both planning, or deciding how to allocate resources, and control, or monitoring the results to ensure they conform with the plan."[7] Planning, budgeting, organizing, and serving are key activities that should be seen as important individual elements while at the same time being viewed as interconnected components of an effective management process (see Figure 2).

Traditional vs. Program-Based Budgeting

Even while a number of libraries have placed their decision-making processes within the construct of a planning design, financial management has often remained a fixed accounting process, separate from any defined plan. "For the most part, libraries are budgeting much as they have always done, incrementally from year to year, taking last year's budget, incrementing it, and then modify-

FIGURE 2

Critical Elements of Effective
Planning and Budgeting Processes

Planning
- ▶ Assesses user base.
- ▶ Evaluates internal strengths and weaknesses.
- ▶ Identifies major constraints and opportunities.
- ▶ Builds team spirit.
- ▶ Results in clear, understandable goals.

Budget
- ▶ Flexible.
- ▶ Identifies accountability.
- ▶ Supports organizational plan.
- ▶ Reflects library programs and priorities.
- ▶ Promotes consideration of alternatives.

ing it where appropriate or necessary."[8] The traditional line item budget that is in use today in many libraries is primarily an accounting system that calls for a review of annual expenditures for the year and a projection of costs in broad categories (lines) for the following year (see Figure 3). Cost requirements for specific programs are not determined. Instead, items such as salaries and wages, books, supplies, etc., are used across the institution. This approach to budgeting in today's libraries inhibits innovative design and creative execution of library programs through a fixed system that promotes incremental allocation to all parts of the budget without review, accountability, or relationship to the priorities of the guiding plan. In using planning principals to respond in a rational way to a variety of pressures, the financial support systems for library operations must be a critical part of the planning picture, integrated into the programs of the library. While the traditional resource and expenditure budgeting process has served us well as an accounting system, it has frequently held us hostage to its "who spent how much for what" format.

For the challenges of the present and the future we need a budget that is based on the programs of the library, one that allows creative

FIGURE 3

Sample Line Item Account Summary

	Budget	Current Month	Current Year	Encumbrances	Bal
Salaries					
Student Wages					
Benefits					
Supplies and Services					
Data Processing					
Books, Periodical, Binding					

review of those programs within the context of the overall plan and the library's goals and objectives. The system must permit us to consider alternatives and place accountability at the level where it correctly belongs. An effective budgeting system allows us to be creative in deciding the most effective method of serving our users. "Change in library management is now the order of the day. Budgeting–resource management–and creativity–fostering environments which encourage questioning, divergent thinking and new ways of looking at things–are our most powerful tools as we move toward the 21st century."[9] Rather than a traditional listing of how much money is being spent on what service, we need to know not only what is being spent but to what purpose; which programs we are supporting and to what extent. Effective management requires a budget process that is a reflection of the goals of the library and its institution or governing board, one that shows in monetary terms the priorities of the overall plan, and one that is flexible, allowing for alternatives. "A budget is a quantitative expression of a plan of action and an aid to coordination and implementation."[10] Further, it is a key public relations tool, a defining statement of organizational priorities, and a critical component in creative management.

The Elements of a Program-Based Budget

In order to respond effectively in an environment of shrinking dollars, increasing needs of a changing clientele, inflationary costs, and changing technology for library and information resources, we require a financial support system that communicates clearly, links financial support with identified programs and priorities, promotes the consideration of alternatives, and assigns some accountability for management of service and support programs to those responsible for carrying them out. We need a system that allows us to analyze what it is we are doing in light of our goals and objectives and permits us to review possibilities and change course when necessary. What is needed is a budget system that reflects the organizational plan in the disbursement of financial resources to the program priorities of the library. "The merits of program budgeting are both real and substantial . . . The principal theoretical advantage of program budgeting is that it links together the organization's inputs (the resources, typically dollars deployed) and outputs, goals, objectives, products, programs, etc. By contrast, in traditional incremental budgeting, the inputs tend to increase space, while the priority ranking of the outputs may change substantially over time, with consequent progressive deterioration of the fit between inputs and outputs–disjointed incrementalism. In short, program budgeting helps ensure that the organization's resources are deployed where they will produce the greatest benefit to the organization. Program budgeting theoretically forces an examination of the organization's goals and objectives and the fit between them and its programs; it can also examine the fit between programs and deployment of resources. If used properly, program budgeting has the potential to turn the budgeting process into a much more rational, interactive process and to make the budgeting process correspondingly less arbitrary and less whimsical."[11]

Formal techniques for program budgeting have been developed and are in use in the business community, most frequently under the headings "Program Planning Budgeting System" (PPBS) and "Zero-Based Budgeting." PPBS, commonly used in the Defense Department in the 1960s, calls for the creation and review of alternatives to determine the most effective means of meeting established goals. Outcomes must be quantifiable and are evaluated according to their impact on goals and objectives. Zero-Based Budgeting, developed at Texas Instruments in the 1970s, begins each year anew and calls for justifying needs for funding requests rather than building upon any previously established amounts. It stresses justifying each program with the beginning of the new year. While these formal program budget systems are effective methods for arranging priorities and outcomes and assigning financial resources, they are very formalized and may not be the most effective method for planning and allocating the budget. Regardless of the actual format chosen, a budget system should stem from the organizational plan and serve as a key part of the operation.

Using budgets which are based upon the library's programs allows one to identify major activities undertaken by the library to achieve particular goals, indicate priorities, assign responsibility, and define expected outcomes. The budget emanates from library goals and objectives which are established within the context of the vision that the library has for itself. Programs are defined as major tasks the library undertakes to fulfill its mission. Activities are carried out within single or multiple program areas to achieve the objectives established for the program. A program-based budgeting process allows you to plan within the foundation of the goals and objectives, prepare clear and careful delineation of programs, allocate appropriate resources based upon priorities with concomitant flexibility, review and defend or question spending for each program, evaluate expenditures in relation to the established plan, and consider alternatives in light of changing conditions (see Figure 4).

The planning process, the budgetary system and the organizational structure should form a unified approach to management. The effective program-driven budget translates the library's plans into financial priorities. At a time of dramatic change and increased accountability, a budget system that is linked to the programs of the library provides the financial flexibility necessary to respond to these challenges. "Librarianship . . . at least historically, has not been a context where substantial diversity of alternatives has existed. As has been pointed out, it is only comparatively recently that librarianship has entered the stage at which the technology on which the field is based has been growing more rapidly than the problems to be addressed and therefore capable of providing real alternatives. An obvious ramification is that as electronic technology races ahead, the library will become increasingly dynamic, increasingly susceptible to widely diverging alternatives, and budgeting techniques that facilitate the evaluation of alternatives will become more relevant."[12]

THE CHALLENGE OF IMPLEMENTING A PROGRAM-BASED BUDGET

The purpose of program budgeting is easier to articulate than the implementation of the budget process itself. Typically, institutions that have not converted to a program-based budget in the past have been inhibited from doing so for a number of reasons: (1) a management style (either within the parent institution, the board or the library itself) which favors centralized budget control; (2) a budget system imposed by external forces (e.g., the parent institution, the board, the state); (3) the lack of internal resources or knowledgeable

FIGURE 4

Sample Program-Based Resource Report

	Budget	Current Month	Current Year	Encumbrances	Balance
Administration					
Salaries					
Wages					
Supplies					
Automation					
Operations					
Equipment					
Salary Savings					
Automated Systems					
Salaries					
Wages					
Supplies					
Automation					
Operations					
Equipment					
Salary Savings					
Collections					
Salaries					
Wages					
Acquisitions					
Supplies					
Equipment					
Automation					
Operations					
Equipment					
Salary Savings					
Public Services					
Salaries					
Wages					
Supplies					
Automation					
Operations					
Equipment					
Salary Savings					
Technical Services					
Salaries					
Wages					
Supplies					
Automation					
Operations					
Equipment					
Salary Savings					

individuals to develop a program budget; and (4) the absence of a strategic planning process which would stress the importance of budgeting linked to programs. For libraries without such a budgeting system, it is also likely that staff have never had the responsibility for helping to develop the budget or being held accountable for budget tracking and expenditures. Thus, conversion to a program-based budget also implies staff development to prepare individuals who have not been involved in budgeting in any major way to assume responsibility for budget planning and execution.

Management Style

Until the 1960s when faculty status and participatory management became popular management styles in libraries, directors and deans tended to exercise tight centralized budget control. Often the budget process was something of a mystery to staff. They simply made proposals that were funded or turned down. Even with the advent of participatory management as a recognized approach to library decision-making during the last two decades, this has not necessarily translated into changes in budget management. Because most libraries (even those with faculty status for librarians) function hierarchically and accountability still rests with the dean or director, budget control has continued to be highly centralized. Individuals, committees or task forces recommend to the dean or director, but final distribution of resources has remained tightly controlled. Therefore, need for more effective budgeting has emanated less from external forces than from the articulated vision of the director or dean as internal allocation decisions are made. Even where "Management by Objectives" (MBO) was widely used by governmental bodies in the 1970s and early 1980s, the process for setting those objectives and tying funding to the objectives seldom evolved from a strategic planning process; they were much more likely to have been established administratively. For example, in Iowa, the state legislature still requires that each state university start the budget process with less than 100 per cent of its previous budget and rationalize why it needs the additional funding, a version of MBO. The response to this request is usually provided by the university budget officer, not the primary units of the university. The rationale provided may be taken from unit strategic plans, but there is no guarantee of that. In fact, internal library plans may have changed significantly and not be reflected in the response to the state which is based on the previous year's budget discussions. Also, as these documents rise through the bureaucracy, they tend to become more and more succinct, with bulleted items summarizing entire sections of original documents.

Institutional Constraints

Since libraries are usually part of a larger parent organization, and that parent organization may be part of a larger governmental body, it is generally the case that an external budget system is required. That system is not likely to be based on library programs; and even if it is, it may not suit the internal requirements of the library in structuring its own effective budget system. The challenge to library management is to investigate whether the prescribed budget format can be adapted to also function as a program budget. This requires learning the structure of the given budget system in detail and working within the constraints of that system design.

Internal Resources

Conversion from a line item budget to a budget based on library programs is not a trivial process. At minimum, it requires an individual within the library who has the ability to analyze the format of the old budget system and to reformulate it into a new structure. Since the old budget system probably does not aggregate information in the categories that a program-based budget will require, data must either be re-analyzed from the previous year and re-categorized; or alternatively the new system must be set up and data captured during the year so that at the end of the first year, there will be a year's worth of actual expenditures to guide budget distribution the next year. If the overall budget system of the institution or governing body cannot be used as a program budget, it is possible that a parallel internal system will have to be adopted. It is important to minimize that effort so as not to duplicate the workload of maintaining two systems. It is preferable to develop an internal system that reformulates the transactions to mirror the institutional budget. That will require programming skills within the library and careful analysis of workflow within the budget department.

Strategic Planning and Budget Development

Strategic planning, by whatever name, is increasingly common if not mandated. However, there are still many libraries that have not experienced a formal strategic planning process and have therefore not created a formal internal plan that can be used as the basis for a program budget. Where that is the case, the organizational structure of the library can be used as a form of program budget, whereby the budget is set up around major functions. Even where a strategic plan does exist, you must decide how detailed a budget is required (see Figure 5). Too much detail may actually inhibit flexibility, as a

FIGURE 5

Detail of Sample Program-Based Resource Report

	Budget	Current Month	Current Year	Encumbrances	Balance
Public Services					
Reference					
Salaries					
Wages					
Supplies					
Automation					
Operations					
Equipment					
Salary Savings					
Bibliographic Instruction					
Salaries					
Wages					
Supplies					
Automation					
Operations					
Equipment					
Salary Savings					
Access Services					
Salaries					
Wages					
Supplies					
Automation					
Operations					
Equipment					
Salary Savings					

change in priorities may require major transfers across budget lines. One of the virtues of the old line item budget is simplicity.

Staff Development

An effective budgeting system is a well communicated one that depends upon staff participation. Yet in libraries that have had highly centralized budget control, staff will not have experience with the budget process. More important, they will not have any experience being held accountable for presenting proposals with detailed budget analysis included nor with monitoring and adhering to a budget once allocations are made. They will be more accustomed to a top-down approach to resource allocation and tracking. In a transition to a new budget system, staff may need training through workshops or seminars in budget construction and monitoring. Critical to this process, is the psychological acceptance of responsibility. In the long-run, most staff prefer to understand the system and to have the opportunity of making the system work to accomplish their goals. But in the short-term, they will often revert to the older mentality and will want reassurance that they are on the right track.

IMPLEMENTATION STRATEGIES

Conversion of a line item to a more program-based format usually requires several stages:

- Determination of program/budget priorities;
- Analysis of current budget system and flexibility;
- If the existing budget system is too inflexible to be converted to a new format, selection of other software or decision about internal programming;
- Categorization of budget data into program format;
- Re-tallying of previous year data into new budget categories to see how funds have been expended in the past, as a guide to new allocations; or alternatively, capture of this year's expenditures in new categories as guide to next year's allocations;
- Annual review thereafter to update strategic plan and to formulate next year's budget priorities in line with program priorities.

An example of this process is under way at Iowa State University. The new Dean of Library Services took office on July 1, 1989. Prior to that date the university and the library had a very centralized budget system and decision-making process. The library budget used a line item format of six categories. While it produced a fairly good accounting of library expenditures in broad, library-wide categories, it did not identify priorities or responsibilities and it was difficult to know how much was being spent on different functions, programs, or services within the library.

In 1989, under a new provost and president, the university adopted decentralized budgeting under a new program called "block budgeting," whereby deans and directors of academic units had a great deal of freedom in reallocating funds internally once annual budget allocations were made to their units. Simultaneously, the academic units of the university underwent a mandated strategic planning process; and the library was successful in being included in that process. Thus, now the library has a strategic plan and an annual process for updating that plan as part of the annual budget process.

Phase one of converting to a more effective system, then, was to begin to plan an internal format using a microcomputer-based database management system. The programming was to be done by a senior member of the library systems office who had considerable experience with budget systems. Just as the library staff was to begin this effort in 1991, the university announced that it intended to revamp its automated accounting system, including major revision of internal accounting codes. It was also made clear that the university administration wished units to minimize duplication of effort implied by parallel systems. The alternative, therefore, was to become more conversant with the proposed system and to try to utilize it to simulate a budget emphasizing library programs.

In looking at how academic colleges set up their budgets, it appeared that major functional areas in the library could be established to emulate academic departments within colleges. The new accounting codes could be used within these functional areas so that we could track and cross-tabulate types of transactions across library functional areas to see how much we were spending collectively by area and by type of transaction (e.g., salaries, equipment, automation) to guide allocations for the next fiscal year (1993/94).

Stage two of the implementation process breaks the library budget out by major functional areas–the five divisions of the library: administration, public services, technical services, systems, and collections.

Because funds have not been tracked this way in the past, we estimated expenditures in the new categories for the previous year in order to establish the new budget. Because it was too labor-intensive to retabulate many types of expenditures, such as equipment and supplies, by the new categories, those funds were left in a central pool for the 1992/93 budget year; but new program categories were established in the budget as well. Equipment expenditures, for example, will be transferred to the actual program area during the year so that actual expenditures will be available by the end of the fiscal year to guide next year's allocations. Certain costs that were easy to reallocate by program area, such as telephones and staff, were assigned by program within this year's budget. Because supplies are purchased centrally in bulk and sometimes allocated from a central inventory over several years, it appeared very difficult to track purchase of supplies in the new format. Instead, an internal microcomputer-based distribution program was implemented that tracks actual allocation of supplies during the year. This can be used to question patterns of expenditure by program area but is not integrated into the order and expenditure budget process, which remains a line item within the administrative program. This is an example where an internal decision has to be made as to the level of detail needed at the program level.

With the exception of supplies, which can be approximated through the allocation system, all expenditures will be allocated and trackable by library function by the end of this current fiscal year. The third phase of developing a new budget system will be to determine whether to track even more specific programs within divisions next year, for example OCLC costs within division, bibliographic instruction within the public services units, etc. It is possible to do this within the university system, but it is cumbersome. A decision will have to be made about what level of program accountability is reasonable and necessary to match expenditures to priorities established by the strategic and annual review process. The more detailed the system, the more labor-intensive are the bookkeeping transactions required.

SUMMARY

Resource management is a critical component of library service. In order to be an effective tool, it must flow from the plan of operation and reflect the program priorities of the library. Effective budget control encourages creativity, assigns responsibility, and permits review of alternatives and is sensitive to the requirements of the organization as it works to meet user needs. The successful budget system is responsive to organizational changes and new program directions called for by the planning process. Whatever form of program-based budgeting is adopted, it must meet these goals for an effective resource management system with the resulting effect being the promotion of responsive and meaningful user service.

NOTES

1. Bertha R. Almagro, "Budgeting and Planning: A Tandem Approach," *Serials Librarian* 10 (Fall 1985 - Winter 1986): 173-9.
2. Michael E. D. Koenig and Deirdre C. Stam, "Budgeting and Financial Planning for Libraries," in *Advances in Library Administration and Organization* 4 (1985): 77-110.
3. Carla Stoffle, "Funding and Creativity, Part I: Funding," *Bulletin of ASIS* 17 (December 1990/January 1991): 16-18.
4. Meredith Butler and Hiram Davis, "Strategic Planning as a Catalyst for Change in the 1990s," *College and Research Libraries* 53, no.5 (September 1992) 393-403.
5. For an excellent discussion of strategic planning and the role of libraries in the process, see James F Williams, II, ed., "Strategic Planning in Higher Education," *Journal of Library Administration* 13, nos. 3,4 (1990).
6. Stoffle, op. cit.
7. Lauren Kelly, "Budgeting in Nonprofit Organizations," *Drexel Library Quarterly* 21 (Summer 1985): 3-18.
8. Michael E.D. Koenig and Victor Alperin, "ZBB and PPBS: What's Left Now That The Trendiness Has Gone?" *Drexel Library Quarterly* 21 (Summer 1985): 19-38.
9. Carla Stoffle, "Funding and Creativity, Part II: Creativity," *Bulletin of ASIS* 17 (February/March 1991): 21-23.
10. Koenig and Stam, op. cit.
11. Stoffle, op. cit.
12. Koenig and Alperin, op. cit.

Index

Accident rate, of older workers, 147
Accountability
  in budgeting, 178
  in higher education, 92,93,172
Adler, Alfred, 8
Administrative occupations, job growth in, 110
Affirmative action, 15-16
Age Discrimination in Employment Act, 146,149
Aggressiveness, as male characteristic, 114
Aging
  of population, 40. *See also* Older workers
  of workforce, 145-149
ALCTS, Policies Planning Committee of Collection Management and Development Section, 161,163,164,166,167
American Association for Higher Education, 91
American Association of Retired Persons, 146
American Library Association, library school accreditation by, 44-45,50-51,61
Americans with Disabilities Act, 41
Architecture, organizational, 123
Association of College and Research Libraries, statement on library education, 168-169

Baby-boom generation, 146
Behavioral competence, training for, 138-140

Besemer, Susan, 74,75,79
Bibliographic access
  by catalog, 55
  by faculty, 160
Bibliographic instruction programs, 26-27
Bifocals, use by older workers, 155
Brain, hemispheric lateralization of, 61-62
Budget, 171-88
  accountability in, 178
  line-item, 177
    conversion to program-based budgeting, 183
    versus progam-based budget, 176-178,179
  program-based, 178-188
    case example of, 186-187
    elements of, 178-180,181
    implementation of, 180,182-187
    incremental budgeting versus, 176-178,179
    institutional constraints on, 183
    internal resources for, 180,182,183
    management style and, 180,182-183
    obstacles to, 180,182
    staff involvement in, 185
    strategic planning and, 182,184-185
  Program Planning Budgeting System, 179
  as public relations tool, 178
  Zero-Based, 179
Budgeting, definition of, 175

© 1993 by The Haworth Press, Inc. All rights reserved.

Budget management
  by collection development
    librarians, 161-164
  for older workers, 157
Bureaucracy, 71,119,120

Cadillac, 95
California, minority-dominated
    population of, 40
Carothers, Robert, 96
Carpal tunnel syndrome, 154-155
Cataloging, networking in, 151
Chaffee, Ellen Earle, 95-96
Chairs, ergonomics of, 154
Change. *See also* Organizational
    change
  factors promoting, 171-173
  implications for library education,
    39-54
  older workers' resistance to,
    152,155
    change management for,
      156-157,158
  technological, 55,149-152,172
Change management, for older
    workers, 156-157,158
Change strategies
  empowerment as, 3-18
    consequences of, 11-16
    ego development theory of,
      8-11
    factors influencing, 8-11
    organization theory and, 6-8
    participative management
      versus, 4-6
  organizational politics and, 134
Collaboration. *See also* Networking
  in collection development, 56
  computing center-library, 165-166
  interorganizational, 33,132-133
    organizational boundaries and,
      120
    as organizational development
      goal, 135-136
  intraorganizational, 119

COLLDV-L, 161,162,164,166,167
Colleagues, leader's relationship
    with, 117,120,121
Collection development, cooperative,
    56
Collection development librarian,
    159-170
  budgeting role of, 161-164
  educational and professional
    preparation of, 167-169
  future trends affecting, 159-162
  information technology expertise
    of, 164-166
  mentoring programs for, 167
Communication
  by leaders, 122
  within the library organization, 67
  in team management,
    77,78,79,80,81,82
  worker-supervisor, 79
Communication skills, of librarians, 47
Compensatory theory, of power, 8
Competition
  empowerment and, 13,14
  in higher education, 92-93,105
  as male characteristic, 112
  rewards for, 13
  among staff, 25
  time-based, 123
Computer systems, upgrading of,
    150-152
Computer workstation, for older
    workers, 153-155
Computing centers, collaboration
    with libraries, 165-166
Congruity, of leaders, 117
Constancy, of leaders, 117,118
Continuing education, 168
  for organizational change, 138
Control chart, 105
Core competence strategy, 123
Creativity, 60-62
  in library management, 175,178
  obstacles to, 61
  risk taking and, 66

Crosby, Philip, 96,98
Cultural diversity, 40
  implications for librarians, 47-48
Cultural factors, in empowerment, 11
Culture, organizational, "feminine" nature of, 122
Customers, in total quality management, 97,99-101

Databases, OPAC access to, 55
Defensiveness, 33-34
Deming, W. Edwards, 96-97,98,101,102
Democracy
  of female leaders, 113
  in the workplace, 3,7,97
Devaluation, 71,171-172
Developmental tasks, gender differences in, 10-11
Dickinson College Library, 70
Director
  budget management role, 182
  female, 109
  risk-taking role, 66
  strategic planning role, 59,60
Discrimination, age-related, 146
Disney, Walt, 58
Doctorate, in library science, 45-46
Dorsey, Sarah, 79-83
Drucker, Peter, 97

Education. *See also* Higher education; Library and information science education
  trends in, 42
Ego development
  empowerment and, 8-11
  of managers, 15
Electronic library, 43-44,160-161
  collection development librarians' role in, 164-166
Electronic list services, 161-162

Electronic mail, 67
Employees. *See* Staff
Empowerment
  in automobile industry, 124
  cultural factors in, 11
  definition of, 4
  effect on job turnover rate, 13,14-15
  by leaders, 118
  as library function, 21
  manager's qualities for, 15
  as self-efficacy, 5-6,7,11,12-13,14-15
  of staff, 3-18,135
  as strategy for change, 3-18
    consequences of, 11-16
    ego development theory of, 8-11
    factors influencing, 8-11
    organization theory and, 6-8
    participative management versus, 4-6
Ergonomics, of the workplace, 153-155
Erikson, Erik, 8-9
Executive occupations, job growth in, 110

Faculty
  attitudes towards librarians and libraries, 161,166
  bibliographic access by, 160
Failure, fear of, 5
Family structure, changes in, 40-41
  implications for library service, 48
Federal Express, 95
Fifth Discipline: The Art and Practice of the Learning Organization (Senge), 21-37
Financial factors. *See also* Budget; Funding
  affecting higher education, 92,93
  affecting libraries, 71,171-172

Fishbone diagram, 105
Flexibility, of leaders, 116-117
Flex time, 41,148,149
Flow chart, 104-105
Foreign languages, in school curriculum, 42
Fox Valley Technical College, total quality management at, 94-95,106
Freud, Sigmund, 8-9
Friedan, Betty, 58
Funding
  reductions in, 42,56
  for risk-taking endeavors, 66

Games Mother Never Taught Me (Harragan), 111
Gardening, as leadership metaphor, 65
General Motors, Saturn plant of, 124
Generativity, 10
Globalization, 41-42
Goals
  of academic libaries, 25-26
  in behavioral competence development, 139
  in organizational transformation, 21,139
  in program-based budgeting, 179,180
  in strategic planning, 59-60,175
  in total quality management, 103

Habermas, Jurgen, 7
Handbook of Leadership (Bass), 111-112
Harmon, Michael, 7
Harvard Business Review, 63-64,112
Helping behavior, as empowerment strategy, 10
Higher education
  forces for change in, 92-93
  trends in, 42

Hispanics
  population growth rate of, 40
  school enrollment of, 42
Histogram, 105
Horney, Karen, 8
Human resources. *See also* Older workers; Staff
  investment in, 3
  organizational importance, 13
  in total quality management, 102
Hummel, Ralph, 7

Immigrants, in workforce, 41
In a Different Voice: Psychological Theory of Women's Development (Gilligan), 10
Inferiority complex, 8
Inflation, 71,171-172
Information counselor, librarian as, 48-49
Information systems, user-friendly, 27
Information technology
  implications for collection development librarians, 164-166
  effect on library organization structure, 43
  in library school curriculum, 45
  effect on workplace, 41
Innovation, by substitution, 62-63
Integrity, of leaders, 118
Internet, 25,55,151
Intimacy development, 10
Intrapreneurship, 63,67
  funding of, 66
Iowa State University, budget system of, 182-183,186-187
Ishikawa, Kaoro, 96,97,98
ITT, 98

Janis, Irving, 119
Japan, total quality management in, 96-98,103

Job design, empowerment's effect on, 16
Job turnover rate
　empowerment's effect on, 13,14-15
　of older workers, 147,149
Journals. *See* Serials
Juran, Joseph M., 96,97-98,102

Kehoe, Dalton, 100
King, Martin Luther, Jr., 58
Kittle, Barbara, 76-79

Leaders
　controlling approach of, 24
　in learning organizations, 36-37
　relationship with colleagues, 117,120,121
　relationship with staff, 117,118,123,124
　successful, 115-118
　as teacher, 36-37
　of total quality management teams, 102
　transformational, 20-21,55-68
　　communication style of, 67
　　comparison with managers, 57
　　creativity of, 60-62,67
　　"futures-creative," 58
　　innovativeness of, 62-63
　　as intrapreneur, 63,67
　　qualities of, 115-118
　　risk taking by, 65-66
　　strategic planning by, 58-60
　　women as, 112-113
　transitional, 20
　vision of, 21,74,115-117,118,124
　　lack of, 24-25
　　in learning environments, 36-37
　　shared, 23,32-33,34-35,36-37
Leaders (Bennis), 110
Leadership style
　　empowerment and, 13
　　"feminine," 122
　　gender differences in, 63-65,109-128,111-114
　　gender-specific characteristics and, 111-113
　　socialization and, 111
　　organizational development and, 135-136
　　in team management, 73-76,77,78-79
　　values model of, 120-122,124
Learning organization model, of management, 21-37,122
　definition of, 22
　"five discipline" theory of, 21-37
　　building shared visions, 23,32-33,34-35,36-37
　　leader's role in, 36-37
　　mental models, 23,31-32
　　personal mastery, 22,29-31,35
　　systems thinking, 22,26-29
　　team learning, 23-24,33-34
Librarians
　male, 109,111
　minority-group, 56
　skills and abilities required of, 46-49
　subservient self-image of, 24
Librarianship
　male leadership of, 109
　as women's profession, 109,110-111
Libraries. *See also* Research libraries
　future trends in, literature survey of, 159-162
　as network, 164
Library and information science education
　American Library Association-accredited, 44-45,50-51,61
　changes affecting, 39-54
　　accreditation standards, 50-51
　　curriculum changes, 45,50
　　faculty composition changes, 45-46,50
　　implications of, 46-49

library changes, 43-44
school closings, 44
social change, 39-42
creativity in, 61
Library users, diversity of, 47-48
Linear thinking, as organizational limitation, 24
Longevity, trends in, 145-146

MacArthur, Douglas, 96-97
Mainframe computer systems, upgrading of, 150-151
Malcolm Baldridge award, 95
Management
    "collegial," 70
    as librarians' skill, 47
    by objective, 182-183
    participatory
        budget management implications of, 182
        empowerment versus, 4-6
        program-based budgeting and, 180,182-183
    scientific, 119
    team approach in, 140-141
Manager
    distinguished from leader, 57,114-115
    empowerment role, 15
    female, 109,110
    networking by, 133
    personal conflict involvement of, 27
    power orientation of, 15
    relationship with staff, 97
    training of, 139-140
Managerial occupations, job growth in, 110
Martin Corporation, Pershing Missile project at, 98
Master of library science degree programs
    American Library Association-accredited, 50-51,61
    discontinuation of, 44
    increased access to, 44-45
    Association of College and Research Libraries statement on, 168-169
    content of, 167-169
    as partial professional preparation, 168-169
Maturing workers. *See* Older workers
McClelland, David, 8-10,12,15
Mental models, 23
    management of, 31-32
    microcomputers and, 35-36
Mentoring, as empowerment strategy, 12
Microcomputer, for microworld modeling, 35-36
Microworld, 35-36
Minority groups
    as librarians, 56
    population growth rates of, 40
    school enrollment of, 42
Mission statement, 59
Moral development, of women, 10-11
Motorola, 95

Napoleon Bonaparte, 58
National Association of College and University Business Officers, 91-92,100
National Research and Education Network, 151
Network, library as, 164
Networking
    in cataloging, 151
    by managers, 133
Newsletter, library-wide, 67
Niles, Carrie, 74-76,79
North Dakota State University System, total quality management use by, 95-96,106
NREN, 25

Objectives
  in program-based budgeting,
    179,180
  in strategic planning, 59-60,175
OCLC terminal, 150
Older persons, as college students, 42
Older workers
  accident rate of, 147
  age-related abilities decline of,
    148-149
  creativity of, 148
  productivity of, 147-149,153
  resistance to change by, 152,155
    change management for,
      156-157,158
  stereotypes of, 146-147
  in technical services, 145-158
    budget implications of, 157
    change management for,
      156-157,158
    change resistance of, 152,155
    ergonomic considerations for,
      153-155,157,158
    technological innovation and,
      149-152
    training of, 155-156,157,158
  turnover rate of, 147,149
  work attendance by, 147
Online public access catalog
  (OPAC), 55
*On Q: Causing Quality in Higher
  Education* (Seymour),
  92,93
Oregon State University, total quality
  management at, 95,99,106
Organizational change
  external pressure-related, 92
  in higher education, 92-93
  rate of, 27-28
  in research libraries, 129-143
    generality in, 131-132
    integrative mechanisms in,
      132-133,136
    organizational culture/values
      in, 133-134

organizational politics and,
  134-136
strategic planning versus,
  136-137
training versus, 138-140
Organizational development
  definition of, 130
  function of, 140
  organizational politics and, 135-136
  value orientations of, 134
Organizations
  bureaucratic, 71,119,120
  changing models of, 118-125
  limitations of, 24-25
Organization theory, relationship to
  empowerment, 6-8
Out of the Crisis (Deming), 70

Pareto chart, 105
Performance attainment, 5
Personal computer. *See also*
  Microcomputer
  technological improvements of, 150
Personal mastery, 22,29-31,35
Persuasion, verbal, 5
Peterson, Donald, 97
Philip Crosby and Associates, 98
Planning
  budget use in, 171-188
    case example of, 186-187
    elements of, 178-180,181
    implementation of,
      180,182-187
    incremental budgeting versus,
      176-178,179
    institutional constraints on, 183
    internal resources for,
      180,182,183
    management style and,
      180,182-183
    obstacles to, 180,182
    staff involvement in, 185
    strategic planning and,
      182,184-185
  components of, 176

Planning review, 175
Pluralism, cultural, 40
Politics, organizational, 134-136
Population
    aging of, 40. *See also* Older
        workers
    demographic composition of, 40
Population growth, 40
Post-industrial society,
        organizational frontier of,
        139
Power
    compensatory theory of, 8
    of leaders, 118
    need for, 8
    in organizational politics, 134-135
Power orientation, stages of,
    8-11,12,15
Problem-solving
    cause-and-effect in, 28
    in total quality management,
    102,103-104
Process flow diagram, 104-105
Productivity, of older workers,
    147-149
Public library services, traditional
        versus electronic, 43-44
Public relations, budget as tool in,
    178

Quality is Free (Crosby), 98

Reengineering, 122-123
Reliability, of leaders, 117
Repetitive strain injuries, in older
        workers, 154-155
Research libraries
    book orientation of, 131
    goals of, 25-26
    organizational change in, 129-143
        generality in, 131-132
        integrative mechanisms in,
        132-133,136

        organizational culture/values
        in, 133-134
        organizational politics and,
        134-136
        strategic planning versus,
        136-137
        training for, 138-140
Resource management
    accountability in, 172
    budget control in, 171-188
    decision-making for, 65-66,176
Resource sharing, 56
Responsibility, staff's fear of, 12
    as absenteeism cause, 14
Retirement age, 146
Retraining
    increasing need for, 41
    of older workers,
    155-156,157,158
Risk taking, 65-66,116,117
Role modeling, 35
    for empowerment, 12
Run chart, 105

Scale of Moral Development, 10-11
Scatter diagram, 105
School enrollment, increase in, 42
Self-disclosure, 33-34
Self-efficacy, empowerment as,
    5-6,7,11,12-13,14-15
Self-sacrifice, 11
Serials
    increasing budgets for, 26
    increasing cost of, 56,71
Sex-identity characteristics, of female
        and male leaders, 111-113
Seymour, Daniel, 101
Single-parent households, 40-41
Socialization
    effect on leadership qualities, 111
    inot librarianship, 48
Social learning theory, of
    self-efficacy, 5
Staff
    budget-related reduction of, 56

budget system involvement of, 185
competition among, 25
diversity of, 56
empowerment of, 3-18,135
fear of responsibility, 12,14
leader's relationship with, 117,118,123,124
organizational security for, 132
relocation to new services, 62-63
as resource, 97
Standards for Accreditation of Masters' Programs in Library and Information Studies 1992, 50-51
State University of New York at Fredonia, Reed College Library, team management at, 72-78
  Director's evaluation of, 83-86
  team composition in, 73
  team leader's evaluation of, 74-76
  team leadership of, 73-76,77
  team members' evaluation of, 76-83
Stereotypes
  of gender-appropriate behavior, 64
  of older workers, 146-147
Strategic planning, 58-60
  budget development and, 184-185,186
  process of, 173-175
  strategic organizational change versus, 136-137
Strategy, definition of, 59-60
Systems thinking, 22,26-29

Team building, 35,81,140-141
Team learning, 23-24
Teamwork approach, 120,133
  in management, 69-89,140-141
    case example of, 72-89
    communication in, 77,78,79,80,81,82
    history of, 69-70
    problem-solving and, 73,75-76,83-85
    team composition in, 73,75
    team leadership in, 73-76,77,78-79
  in total quality management, 102,103
Technical services department
  equipment replacement schedules of, 150
  older workers in, 145-158
    budget implications of, 157
    change management for, 156-157,158
    ergonomic considerations for, 153-155,157,158
    technological innovation and, 149-152
    training, 155-156,157,158
Technological change, 55,172-173
  effect on older workers, 149-152
  rapidity of, 172
Telecommunications, in library school curriculum, 45
Texas Instruments, 179
Textual analysis, online, 55
Thinking
  divergent, 61
  linear, 24
Thor, Linda, 100
Time, as competitive advantage factor, 123
Timing, in risk taking, 65-66
Total quality improvement, 95
Total quality management, 91-108
  application to higher education, 94-96,99-107
  customer emphasis of, 99-101
  implementation plans for, 97,103-104,106-107
  Malcolm Baldridge award for, 95
  exponents of, 96-99
  themes of, 98-99

Tradition, organizational, 116
Training
  of managers, 139-140
  of older workers, 155-156,157,158
  for organizational change, 138-140
  for total quality management, 102
Transformation, organizational, 19-37. *See also* Leaders, transformational
  "five disciplines" theory of, 21-27
  building shared visions, 23,32-33,34-35,36-37
  leader's role in, 36-37
    mental models, 23,31-32
    personal mastery, 22,29-31,35
    systems thinking, 22,26-29
    team learning, 23-24,33-34
  goals in, 21
Turnover rate, of older workers, 147,149

Values
  definition of, 121
  organizational, 122,133-134,137
  of total quality management, 95-96
Values model, of leadership, 120-122,124
Venture capital account, for risk taking, 66
Virtual book, 160,166
Virtual library, 160,166
Vision,
  of leader, 21,74,115-117,118,124
    lack of, 24-25
    in learning environments, 36-37
    shared, 23,32-33,34-35,36-37
    in personal mastery, 30
Vision statement, 59

Winter, Gibson, 7
Women
  leadership role, 109-128
    demographics of, 110-111
    libraries organizational structure and, 118-125
    qualities of, 115-118
  leadership style, 63-65
  moral development, 10-11
  in workforce, 41,109,110
Women's rights movement, 11
Work attendance, by older workers, 147
Workers
  average age of, 146. *See also* Older workers
  power inequality with supervision, 79
Workforce
  aging of, 145-149. *See also* Older workers
  changing composition of, 41
  women in, 41,109,110
Workplace
  changing nature of, 41,120
  democracy in, 3,7,97
  diversity of, 56
  for older workers, 153-155
Work schedule, flexible, 41,148,149

Xerox, 95

Zero-defects approach, to production, 98

For Product Safety Concerns and Information please contact our EU
representative GPSR@taylorandfrancis.com
Taylor & Francis Verlag GmbH, Kaufingerstraße 24, 80331 München, Germany